Universal
Letter
Writer

Universal Letter Writer

by

Andrew Elliot

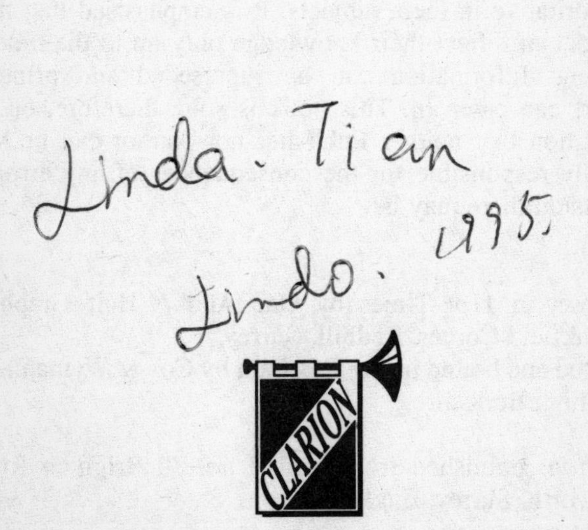

First published by *Clarion* MCMXCV.
Material in this book has been drawn from *Business Letters* and *General & Social Letter Writing*. This edition published by arrangement with Elliot Right Way Books.

Typeset in 11pt Times by One And A Half Graphics, 4 Linkfield Corner, Redhill, Surrey.
Printed and bound in Great Britain by Cox & Wyman Ltd., Reading, Berkshire.

Clarion: published from behind no. 80 Brighton Road, Tadworth, Surrey, England.

Contents

Part 4 – Business Letters

Introduction

The basic principles of letter writing are the same for official business and personal correspondence and to aid the reader this book is in four parts, the first dealing with many general aspects applicable to all kinds of letters.

The second section deals with what is called here "official" correspondence which a private individual would send to a business or institution. Examples range from letters of complaint through to correspondence written when you apply for a job.

The third section deals with social letters to friends, relatives or acquaintances. Get well messages, letters of sympathy and invitations are some of the subjects covered.

The fourth section deals with business correspondence. The business letter can give away much about you and your organisation and is your most important calling card. Whether to increase sales, improve relations with staff, customers, suppliers or the public, well-written letters produce results.

It may be some consolation to those who find difficulty, to know that even the experienced writer is often confronted with a problem and, like the beginner, finds himself staring at paper without a thought or word to put on it. It is useless to sit and look at the paper for a long time, because your mind is apt to become over concentrated on its task; far better to drop the matter for a few hours and come back to it again, when ideas may flow more readily.

I hope that in studying the relevant passages in this book you will find that the ideas required are stimulated, and that each of your letters will make its message clear, and bring home to the recipient all the information he is entitled to expect; in other words an apt, concise, stylistically suitable and competent letter.

Part 1
Letters in General

1
Presentation, Style and Letter Layout

The kind of stationery you use, your style of writing and the way you lay out your letter may say a great deal more about you than your mere choice of words.

Stationery

This section will give you an idea of the different stationery materials available, and includes some personal tips on what you should use, and when.

Paper

The paper you use generally depends on individual taste and the amount of money you wish to spend. There is a wide variety of colours, sizes and qualities of paper from which to choose, and you can also have your stationery personalised with your name, address and other details if you wish.

You should try to avoid using very thin or flimsy paper as it looks cheap. However, when writing to friends abroad, it is a good idea to use lightweight paper and envelopes, as these cost much less to send than ordinary stationery, so you will get more pages for your money! Air mail pads and envelopes are widely available, and special all-in-one aerogrammes can be bought from post offices.

It is always sensible to use a colour of paper which suits the occasion. For instance, you should not really use a bright electric blue or a sunshine yellow paper when sending a sympathy letter or if applying for a job! Paper and envelopes are available in many lovely pastel shades, and if you choose one of these you will not go far wrong.

Although many people use lined paper, I personally

think that a letter written on plain paper always looks more attractive and professional. Many plain writing pads include a lined page for use as a backing sheet, to enable you to get your written lines straight, or you can easily make one up yourself.

If you are concerned about the environment, you may like to buy recycled paper and envelopes which are becoming more widely available.

For information on choosing copy paper, see Keeping Copies Of Correspondence on page 76.

Printed Notepaper

As mentioned earlier, it is possible to have your address specially printed on your notepaper in a wide variety of colours and styles, and there are many high street print shops which can do this for you.

Many people like their printed letterhead to include their name, address and telephone number. For non-business letters it is not really necessary to include your name, as it will appear at the bottom along with your signature; and its inclusion would also prevent other members of the family from using the headed notepaper.

I, personally, would include my telephone number on my printed paper, though some prefer to have the option of writing it on if need be.

Printed notepaper does, undoubtedly, look very attractive, but if you are considering it, my advice would be to keep the design simple, and the words large enough for it to be read easily.

Before going ahead with your printed notepaper, see also Setting Out Your Official Letters and Setting Out Your Social Letters on pages 70 and 131 respectively. Here you will find further advice on the information to include on your headed notepaper, together with ideas on layout.

Labels

Another useful and practical idea is to have your address printed on small, self-adhesive labels. These work out to be fairly cheap; you can have hundreds printed for quite a reasonable price. Again, print shops can do this for you, or they can be bought by direct mail. These are useful for all sorts of purposes – not only for use on letters and postcards, but for identification purposes too (for example, if you lend a book). If you want to use these labels I would advise you to include your name, too, as they will not be used solely for correspondence.

Envelopes

Like paper, envelopes are available in many different sizes, colours and qualities. If you are writing a letter on coloured paper, it always looks better if it is sent in a matching envelope, and that the envelope is big enough for the size of paper you are using. Nothing looks worse than a piece of paper which has been folded several times to make it fit into its envelope!

Many people use smaller envelopes for their personal correspondence, as against the oblong ones used in business, but it really doesn't matter what type is used so long as it is capable of carrying the letter to its destination. That said, however, I wouldn't generally use a cheap manilla envelope for personal letter writing. Nor would I use a cheap envelope, of any kind, for sending out invitations.

When sending air mail letters to friends overseas, it is always a good idea to use a special air mail envelope. That way, there is no chance of it being accidentally sent by sea, when it could take months to arrive.

At post offices you can buy special envelopes for sending letters inland, which have printed on them a first or second class postage mark. It could be useful to have a few of these in reserve in case you run out of stamps and cannot get to a post office.

Cards and Notelets

Many people like to send a special card where they can write a personal note inside, and there is an enormous choice of cards available which carry no printed message in them.

This idea is very similar to sending notelets, which are generally sold in packs of six or ten. They are usually smaller, and work out cheaper, than individual cards and are ideal for writing a short note to a friend.

Postcards

Apart from holiday postcards, this method of communication seems to have gone out of fashion, although postcards do save an envelope and also a little time.

Some people have their name and address printed in small print across the tops of postcards, or they will use a blank postcard with a small self-adhesive address label.

For any brief message, a postcard is ideal, but obviously, it must never be used to convey confidential information.

Writing Materials

Here again, there is a very wide range from which to choose – ball-points, fine-liners, felt-tips, etc. – and many traditionalists still like to use the fountain pen. All these are available in many different coloured inks, so you don't have to stick to the usual black or blue. You could always match your ink to your paper colour, and one very effective combination I have seen is cream coloured paper with brown ink.

Another choice is to type your letters, and for those whose handwriting is not very legible this is ideal.

I always feel that when sending a letter to a business (the bank, for instance) it is better typed, as important information is less likely to be misread, and a typed letter gives a greater feeling of professionalism.

It is often felt that typed personal letters appear less friendly, and I tend to agree. However, for those who are fast typists, it is much quicker to type a letter than to write it, and for long letters to friends, typing would be acceptable. In this case, I would be inclined to make an apology or a joke about the letter being typed, so as to avoid offending anyone.

It should really go without saying that writing letters or addressing envelopes with a pencil is not acceptable. Not only does it look bad, but there is a danger that it could become rubbed out or faded.

If for any reason you *have* to use a pencil because nothing else is available, I would always advise you to apologise for it. There are still many people who would think it very bad taste to receive a letter written in pencil!

Writing Style

There is quite a lot of confusion about style. Many people are not sure what it means. I think a good definition of it would be that it is the manner in which you, as an individual, express your thoughts. Therefore, don't let style be a bugbear to you as it is to many people. I will go further and say that if you have good subject matter, your style will largely look after itself.

Some business people believe that style is essentially the concern of the literateur and that others are, mercifully, not involved but I must emphasise that style makes a great difference to the effect of your letter – and there is no short cut to acquiring the ability to express yourself well.

What might be called the "niceties of style" can, of course, be developed, and are acquired perhaps by the wide reading of experienced authors, noting how, in practice, they express their ideas and thoughts. It requires continual practice to make your sentences and paragraphs flow smoothly. When you read them aloud, notice whether they *sound* satisfactory.

But do not worry too much about style in your everyday social letter writing. Although it will undoubtedly improve a letter, it cannot *make* it; only the ingredients can do that. Remember that what you say matters more than how you say it.

The main function of style, grammar and construction must be to make your writing clear and convey all you wish to say in as few words as possible. Avoid the impression of "heaviness" in your writing at all costs; it does not improve an ordinary letter – in fact it will have the opposite effect.

The main thing to remember about style is to keep your writing simple and straightforward, because anything which is too involved and complicated is bad writing.

Here is an example of muddled style.

Dear Mark,

I have just seen Roger Langton about the forthcoming meeting and he has made various different suggestions about the place and time. We do not know whether the meeting will be large or small but it would probably be best to hold it in the Buckingham Room and Roger thinks the time should be 8.30 not 7.30 otherwise there might not be room for everyone.

Yours sincerely,

You can see at a glance that the writer of the above paragraph did not have clearly in mind what he wanted to convey. Let us analyse sentence by sentence. His first sentence is quite clear, but his second is very muddled; it should read:

We don't know how big the meeting will be, so it will probably be best to hold it in the Buckingham Room, otherwise there might not be enough room for everyone. Roger also thinks that it would be better if we held the meeting at 8.30 instead of 7.30.

This simple example shows the advantage of the short sentence for clarity.

The following example of a muddled sales letter will give the reader some idea of the effect it can have; it provides unlimited scope for misunderstandings:

Dear Mr Smith

I am writing to give you particulars of some 5-drawer filing cabinets which we can offer you at £xxx until the end of the month. I hope you will decide to send a prompt order as these cabinets are selling rapidly and I can guarantee that they are fireproof. As the cost of production of these cabinets is rising you should gain much by buying at this year's price.

We can also supply five dozen hanging files for £www each, which should be sufficient to fill all the drawers amply, and 10 boxes of steel prong fasteners at a special discount price of £yyy all delivered to your premises.

Your order will receive my prompt attention.

Yours sincerely

The same letter reconstructed:

Dear Mr Smith

I am writing to make you a special offer of the following:

1 5-drawer filing cabinet @ £xxx
5 dozen hanging files @ £www
10 boxes steel prong fasteners @ £yyy.

Total cost £zzz, delivered to your premises.* The cabinet is fireproof and is fitted with a safety lock. It is painted in metallic green and there is an A–Z Index for quick referencing.

If you are able to place an order, I shall give it my prompt attention.

Yours sincerely

(*Or if you do not wish to emphasise the grand total, replace this sentence with: "All delivered to your premises.")

Try to get your letter into correct order and if one subject can be made to lead into another, so much the better. In the short letter, where only one or two matters may be dealt with, it is very often a good idea to give a *résumé* in the last line or two, as it holds the recipient's attention to what has already been said. For example:

Dear Mr Lawson

We have now completed the editorial work on the text of your book and I enclose photocopies of all the pages where we have made alterations. I would be grateful if you could read these and let me know whether these minor changes are acceptable.

I also enclose photocopies of some rough illustrations that our cover artist has sketched. Please may we have your opinion on these as well? Within the next week or two, our artist should have completed the line drawings that are to illustrate your text. As soon as he has done so, I will send you photocopies of them all for your approval.

We have tentatively fixed the publication date for 1 September and need to know if this conflicts with any holiday arrangements you might have made.

I look forward to hearing from you soon with regard to the text alterations, cover design and publication date.

Yours sincerely

The last paragraph sums up all the main points of the letter, focusing attention upon them for the benefit of sender and receiver.

Another important point is to avoid using superfluous words and adjectives. In speaking, it is sometimes necessary to repeat what has been said and to use adjectives such as "very" for effect and emphasis, but in writing it is wise to avoid any repetition as far as possible. The reason for this is simply that the written word can be read over again if necessary.

One of the greatest faults of a letter writer is that of pumping one adjective from beginning to end – wonderful day – wonderful food – wonderful beaches. Imagine how irritating a letter of this kind can become. (It's irritating enough if people do this when they're speaking!)

We can all remember being taught at school not to use the same adjective twice in the same sentence or even on the same page, but I feel that this is going a bit too far. Quite often it is not worth changing a word because it has been used a few lines above. Indeed, some writers use deliberate repetition of a word for emphasis, as I have done in the previous paragraph!

I think it is much more important to avoid repetition of information in a sequence of similar words. If you wish to emphasise something it may be necessary to go over the ground again. But use different arguments and try to present the question from a different angle. So, you must not only keep out superfluous words, but, more important, superfluous information. In a social letter this does not mean you should leave out detail, provided it is of interest.

Style alone, in the form of a lot of words correctly put together, can be boring in the extreme. In short – matter, rather than manner, is what matters. (Note repetition of the word matter for effect!)

Have something to write and there will be no need to worry about how to write it. Style comes easily to those who have interesting facts to convey. Qualities such as subtlety of method, lightness in style, and humorous ways of writing can soon be achieved by a little thought and practice, and by studying how they are accomplished by others.

But do not *try* to develop style. Your own is probably far better than any which you may copy. Absorb ideas and layouts from well written books and the classics if you like, but don't consciously imitate them. After all, however badly you may write, the recipient is more interested in you than in your attempts to impress by a style which is not part of you.

There is so much to do these days – and so little time – that the day of the many-paged letter is almost over, except for those who have much time and little to do, or who have friends or relatives who live overseas.

You therefore need a crisp and compact style. One way to help you accomplish this is to study the short leader articles in the popular daily papers, and learn how they achieve effect and grab the interest.

Another method of improving your style is to read lots of the letters which appear in the daily press. These are usually of an extremely high standard, otherwise they would not get printed.

You could also try observing the styles – both good and bad – of letters which are sent to you. This way you will quickly see where you may, in your own writing, be going wrong, or indeed where your correspondents haven't got something quite right!

Letter Layout

Most of us have received letters which began at the far left hand corner of the page, and filled the whole paper without any margins and with very few paragraphs. Not only is the effect of such a letter crowded and messy, but it also makes the contents difficult to understand and follow.

The aim of letter writing is to convey information, and the whole purpose of layout, or construction, is to make the information easily followed by the reader and pleasing to see.

It is, therefore, advisable always to leave about 2cm of margin all round the letter. (This could be reduced to about

1cm if you were using small-sized paper; but no less.) In all letters you should leave enough space between the lines to make them easily read.

There is, however, a bit more to it than this, and for example, in "official" letters or in social letters where you want to stress certain information, there are various hints which you can use.

If you have quite a lot of information to convey, it is a good idea to set it out in numbered points. That way, the reader will more easily be able either to act on the information given, or, if the numbered points are queries, answer each one in turn. Nothing is more annoying than having information or queries overlooked.

This would only really apply to "official" and business letters, as the majority of letters to friends carry information of a social nature. However, if you are arranging a meeting, or something equally important, it is sensible to set this information out in a paragraph of its own.

Paragraphing

Generally speaking, a paragraph is composed of several sentences dealing with the same subject. This, however, must be qualified, because one could write a ten page letter composed of sentences dealing with the same subject. As you can see, one paragraph of such a length would make a letter extremely difficult to follow as well as giving the reader no pause or break. It is, therefore, often a matter of common sense where you break your paragraphs.

As a general guide, you should bear in mind that a paragraph should preferably be not more than about fifteen or at the most twenty lines, with an average of perhaps eight to ten lines as an ideal paragraph length. A letter composed of these average paragraphs is easy to read and follow, but this is only a guide, and there is no fixed rule. A paragraph can vary from between one line to pages in length.

You must, however, avoid starting new paragraphs just

for the sake of it. Equally, you should avoid running two different subjects together because one paragraph may be a little short. In other words, don't be afraid of short paragraphs where necessary. Here is a letter written in paragraphs to show their uses.

Dear Jonathan,

I was so pleased to hear from you, and I'm glad you all had a good holiday. Did you get caught in the traffic on the way back?

Life here has been quite busy lately. We had our annual garden fête last Saturday, with a Fancy Dress Dance at the village hall in the evening.

The weather was lovely for the fête, and we had a good variety of stalls. I was on the plant stall, and I took a lot of cuttings from my greenhouse plants. Old Mr Barker, my next door neighbour, is also a keen gardener and he gave me a lot of plants, so I had a good show.

The Fancy Dress Dance in the evening was absolutely hilarious! Our friend, Peter, went as Tarzan! And I don't mind telling you that his fake-fur leopard skin loin cloth proved to be the life and soul of the party! I wondered if he might start swinging from the village hall rafters after he'd had a few, but he didn't; he just kept beating his chest and doing the "Aargh..." Tarzan call, and eating the bunch of bananas he'd brought!

Sarah went as Cinderella (she looked smashing), and Jeff and I went as the Ugly Sisters! We didn't look quite so smashing – especially after one of Jeff's "balloons" burst when he was dancing with the vicar's wife!

It really was a great evening, and a good time was had by all. We're now back to normal. (Well almost, apart from Ben who went as the Incredible Hulk and is still trying to wash off the green colouring... but that's another story!)

My job has been taking me all over the country lately; in fact, I'll be down your way next Thursday. Would it be

OK to pop in for a cup of tea? I'll give you a call when I'm in your area to see what would be a good time. I expect I'll be finished by about 4 p.m.

Anyway, must finish now so I can cut the hedge before the daylight goes. Hope to see you all next week.

'Bye for now ...

The above shows the use of paragraphs of different length, and although most of the letter is about two subjects – the garden fête and the dance – it illustrates the way in which the different aspects can be separated so that each has its own paragraph.

Note: It is usual in the handwritten letter to indent each paragraph. That means that the first word of a new paragraph is moved in to the right by three or four letter spaces, as in the letter above.

By typesetting convention, the setting out of the remaining letters in this book does not follow this rule. However, it is worth remembering to indent your paragraphs when writing letters by hand, because it makes each paragraph easier to distinguish from the one before.

In typewritten letters indenting can be used, although it is more common nowadays to adopt the fully blocked style without indentation, instead leaving an extra line between paragraphs. The rest of the letters in this book follow this style.

Numbered Paragraphs and Headings

There are many different ways of setting out a letter. In Government offices and Service departments, paragraphs are often numbered to facilitate easy reference. This is in some ways a good idea because it tends to focus the attention of the letter writer on what he is saying and isolates one theme or development of a theme from the next. It is for this reason preferable to separate headings as there may be more than one paragraph under each head.

The disadvantage of this method is its formality and heaviness. There is an alternative, which is particularly suitable when replying to several letters received from one correspondent on the same day. This is to write the letter under successive headings which should be underlined. You may begin your letter by acknowledging all the letters involved, then proceed to the appropriate headings provided by the material.

Numbered headings, or a combination of both these methods, are excellent for long letters dealing with many subjects as they facilitate reply and quick reference.

With shorter letters it is often necessary to use numbered paragraphs or cross headings, but ensure that new paragraphs are made as new subjects are dealt with, or more frequently as necessary.

Reference

When correspondence is large, a simple reference system may be required. Many forms are used, the most common being that in which the initials of the originator and the typist are shown, thus, AGE/MO. Others quote file numbers, contract numbers etc. A long and supposedly imposing reference is nonsense unless all of it has a definite purpose for rapid filing and ease of tracing. One drawback of a long and involved reference is that few correspondents seem able to quote correctly more than four figures or letters at one time, and the objects of the reference are defeated. As a matter of courtesy and helpfulness, always quote a correspondent's reference.

Numbering Letters

Where several letters are sent from the same firm to the same recipient in one day, as in large concerns, a policy of numbering letters may be required to facilitate reference.

Setting out

Most letters (except those to"the Editor") are typed in single spacing. For short letters, use smaller sheets (e.g. A5 paper) or use a larger type size. A letter should not be cramped into a small portion of the page. Conversely, do not spread into two pages when one will do. Also, do not use the reverse of the page unless you are writing a social letter. If using plain paper for continuation sheets, leave four blank lines at the top of the paper, then at the left-hand margin type the number "2" to indicate this is the second page of the letter. On the line below this (still at the left) type the date, and on the next line type the name of your correspondent. Leave another three or four blank lines before continuing the body of the letter. Alternatively, see page 75.

It is most important that every letter you write is dated. The date should appear near the top of the page, either at the left- or right-hand margin, depending on your chosen style. Always type the date in full, i.e. 2 September 1999. This avoids confusion, especially when writing to overseas correspondents who often put the month first when abbreviating the date; for example, to abbreviate 2 September 1999 the Americans would write 9/2/99, while the British would write 2/9/99. Therefore the only way to obviate any problems is to write the date in full.

The simplest way to set out a business letter (and that which is recommended here) is to block everything at the left hand margin. If a reference is included, this can be typed at the left either above or below the date, depending on personal preference, but make sure there is at least one blank line between the reference and date.

Then, again leaving at least one blank line, type the name and address of your correspondent. Below this, leave at least another blank line and type the salutation. The main body of the letter will begin after another blank line, with blank lines being left between paragraphs. At the end of the letter leave one blank line, then type "Yours faithfully" (if you addressed your correspondent as "Dear Sir" or "Dear Madam") or "Yours sincerely" (if you addressed your correspondent by name). Your company name then follows typed in capitals on the line directly below this. Leave about five blank lines for your signature and type your name, and on the line below that, your position in the firm, such as Director, Manager, etc. If the letter is to contain any enclosures, type "Enc" or "Encs" a few lines below this which will remind you to include the relevant papers.

Equal margins either side add to general appearance; nothing looks worse than an uneven, straggling right-hand margin. Remember the importance of first impressions; a neatly laid-out letter gives an impression of efficiency which may have a good effect on the recipient. Similarly, neatness of typing creates a good impression; a letter spattered with alterations gives the reader a feeling he is dealing with someone who is careless and casual. It is better to re-type correctly than to send it out in this state, although for less important letters an odd alteration is permissible.

Signatures should be written in blue or black ink in preference to more startling colours. The latter may be used to stimulate interest, but unfortunately, sometimes it has the reverse effect.

Opposite is an example of a letter set out in the style recommended.

Signed in Absence

A director or partner, or anyone for that matter, may dictate a letter and then have to leave the office before it is typed. In that case, his secretary or a colleague could add the word "for" or the initials "pp" (meaning "per pro" in Latin) beside the sender's name and sign it on his behalf. Alternatively, the following could be typed instead of the sender's name: "Dictated by Mr A B Black and signed in his absence".

BLACK & WHITE LIMITED
1 The Square,
Epsom, Surrey KT1 1XX

Our Ref: ACE/JM

22 February XXXX

The Red River Company Limited
22 Oakehampton Street
Hull
North Humberside
HU11 5ZZ

Dear Sirs

The answer to your letter of 22 January XXXX is that your doors and windows will be delivered to you in the early afternoon of Monday 29 May XXXX.

We assure you we will have someone there to unload them.

With best wishes.

Yours faithfully
BLACK & WHITE LIMITED

John Smith
Director

2

Form and Formalities

Starting the Letter

As well as your own address or business heading, the name and address of the recipient of the letter is included on an official or business letter (at the top left-hand corner immediately above the salutation) in case the envelope becomes defaced; if a copy is taken of the letter, the address will help you, or your typist or filing clerk, to see at a glance to which file it belongs if no other reference system is used. It is sometimes the custom, in more personal letters, to place the recipient's name and address at the bottom left-hand corner.

Salutation and Complimentary Closing of Letters

The opening of a letter and its closing remarks remain a matter of personal taste, *within certain well-defined limits*. All I shall do here is to give some guides and suggestions.

Until recently, most letters passing between large companies began: "Dear Sirs" and ended "Yours faithfully", but nowadays a more personal and friendly note has been introduced. Today, the director of one company will write to the director of another company in quite friendly terms, and the "Dear Sirs" and "Yours faithfully" will be discarded. Instead, he will either write "Dear Mr Smith" or even "Dear John".

On the whole, the rule is that if you don't know the name of the particular individual to whom you are writing, address him as "Dear Sir", or "Dear Madam" if you know it's a woman. But if you are answering a letter you have received, reply to the person who signed the letter, e.g.

"Dear Mr Jones", or "Dear Mrs Smith". After some correspondence (including perhaps telephone conversations and personal meetings) you may progress to being on Christian name terms with your correspondent.

"Yours faithfully" is the accepted business ending to a letter which begins "Dear Sir(s)" or "Dear Madam"; while "Yours sincerely" is the ending for a letter beginning "Dear Mrs Smith" or "Dear John".

One word of warning: business correspondents should avoid becoming too familiar during early acquaintanceship in case the need should ever arise for rather strongly-worded correspondence to pass from one to the other. If, therefore, you have been in the habit of writing "My dear Jack", and then you find yourself in the position of having to dispatch a "Dear Sir, Unless...", you will be in a rather awkward situation. Where your correspondent has attempted to take advantage of your friendly relationship, you may have to revert to the more formal "Dear Sir", and in certain extreme cases, merely the word "Sir".

I would just like to say a word here about one practice which is indulged in and which, although time-consuming, is attractive. It would only be used in an important letter and the idea of it is to convey the extra special personal touch.

The body of the letter is typed in the ordinary way but your secretary leaves the opening line and the closing line blank. You (the writer of the letter) then fill in *in ink* "Dear John" or "Dear Mr Black" or "Dear Sir William" as the case may be and at the end "Yours sincerely", again *in ink*. This tends to lift the letter out of the ordinary.

Forms of Address and Subscription

Fortunately, there is less formality in addressing people of different rank nowadays than there used to be, and much less importance is attached to any minor slip. Nevertheless, it is still courteous to address such people correctly, so I have included the following list. Open punctuation (i.e. not punctuated) is used.

UNTITLED PEOPLE

MAN	Dear Sir or Dear Mr (Mr on envelope)
WOMAN	Dear Madam or Dear Mrs or Dear Miss or Dear Ms (Mrs, Miss or Ms on envelope)
TWO OR MORE MARRIED WOMEN	Dear Mesdames (Mesdames *name* and *name* on envelope)
TWO OR MORE SPINSTERS	Dear Misses (The Misses *name* on envelope)
Two business women can be addressed simply in the salutation of a letter as	Dear Ladies
HUSBAND AND WIFE	Dear Mr and Mrs (no initials or degrees, etc.) (Mr and Mrs on envelope)
BOYS UNDER 14	Dear *Christian name* (Master and *Christian name* on envelope)

The abbreviation for any degrees or qualifications a person may use are put after the name on the envelope, e.g. Mr Peter Jameson, BSc.

You may still find "Esquire" or "Esq" used on the envelope when addressing a man who owns land.

PERSONS OF RANK

	On envelope	*To open and close the letter*
DUKE	His Grace the Duke of	My Lord Duke or Your Grace (refer to as "Your Grace") (I remain, my Lord Duke)
DUCHESS	Her Grace the Duchess of	Madam ("Your Grace") (I remain, Madam)
MARQUIS	The Most Hon. the Marquis of	My Lord Marquis ("Your Lordship") (I remain, my Lord Marquis)
MARCHIONESS	The Most Hon. Marchioness of	Madam ("Your Ladyship") (I remain, Madam)
EARL	The Right Hon. the Earl of	My Lord ("Your Lordship") (I remain, my Lord)
COUNTESS	The Right Hon. the Countess of	Madam ("Your Ladyship") (I remain, Madam)
VISCOUNT	The Right Hon. the (Lord) Viscount	My Lord ("Your Lordship") (I remain, my Lord)
VISCOUNTESS	The Right Hon. the Viscountess, or, The Viscountess	Madam ("Your Ladyship") (I remain, Madam)

	On envelope	*To open and close the letter*
BARON	The Right Hon. Lord, or, The Lord	My Lord ("Your Lordship") (I remain, my Lord)
BARONESS	The Right Hon. the, or, The Baroness	My Lady ("Your Ladyship") (I remain, my Lady)
BARONET	Sir James Milwall Bart. or Bt.	Sir (I am, Sir)
BARONET'S WIFE	Lady Milwall	Madam ("Your Ladyship") (I am, Madam)
KNIGHT	Sir John Newell	Sir (between friends, Dear Sir John) (I am, Sir)
KNIGHT'S WIFE	Lady Newell	Madam (between friends, Dear Lady XX) (I am, Madam)
ARCHBISHOP	His Grace the Archbishop of	My Lord Archbishop ("Your Grace")
BISHOP	The Right Rev. the Lord Bishop of, or The Lord Bishop of	My Lord Bishop ("Your Lordship")
DEAN	The Very Rev. the Dean of	Very Rev. Sir (formal); Mr Dean

	On envelope	*To open and close the letter*
CLERGY	The Rev. William Lockwood (if a Doctor of Divinity, add DD)	Rev. Sir (formal); Dear Sir, Dear Mr, or, if a DD, Dear Dr
JUDGE	The Hon. Mr Justice	Sir
PRIVY COUNCILLORS	The Right Hon. Michael Quarterly MP	Sir (Yours faithfully)
MEMBERS OF PARLIAMENT	Mr David Jones MP Sir Roy Farjeon MP	Sir or Dear Sir (Yours faithfully)
DOCTOR	Dr Peter Ransome	Dear Sir, or, Dear Dr
SURGEON	Mr Philip Palmer FRCS	Dear Sir, or Dear Mr

Commissioned officers of HM Forces are addressed by rank, together with decorations, if any. For Naval officers, add RN. Army officers may have their arm of Service added, e.g. RA, RE.

Replying to Letters

One would hardly imagine it necessary to write a section on answering a letter, but from long experience of replying to correspondence and having my letters answered, I regard this as one of the most important sections of the book.

The first rule about answering a letter is obviously to *ANSWER* it, and this is where so many people go wrong. Frequently in social letters and more often in official and business letters there may be three, six or more different matters for attention. What so often happens is that the reply covers a few of them, but the other points raised are just ignored, which is, to say the least, extremely exasperating for the recipient, who is expecting answers to *all* his queries.

The best way to reply to a letter which raises several points is to have it in front of you, and as you answer the various questions or matters raised you can draw a line through the relative part of the letter. In this way you can see at a glance when you have replied to everything.

It is not always easy, in this busy day and age, to reply to letters by return, but you should try to do so if possible – particularly when dealing with official and business correspondence. This is not just because replying by return gives a good impression, but because there is nothing easier than putting off the writing of a letter, and days of delay are liable to spread into weeks.

Failing a reply by return, a postcard should be dispatched immediately, acknowledging the correspondence and promising an early answer or indicating when one will be sent. Sending a brief card or letter to acknowledge receipt of an important letter will give you time to think carefully about your reply. Where delay is possible, never under-estimate the importance of a day or more's consideration before posting any correspondence which may have serious repercussions. Frequently this will result in the re-writing of the letter or perhaps its cancellation.

Second, always try to put yourself in the place of the recipient to make sure your letter is clear, courteous and avoids annoying the receiver unless, of course, that is your deliberate intention. On this point, I believe that of every one hundred people who write letters to get their own back or to annoy, ninety-nine later regret having done so.

There are other letters which require no reply at all – and here I include the insulting letter which may occasionally be received. Frequently, the wisest course is to ignore the writer. The man or woman who writes a letter to annoy you does so in the hope of succeeding, but only the things which we allow to hurt us do so, and if the insolent communication is merely filed away or put into the waste paper basket, it does no harm.

It is impossible to deal with every conceivable angle of this question of replying to letters, but one very important rule is that if you are ever behind with your payments and receive a letter requesting a settlement, an immediate reply of explanation should be sent. Many firms regard the ignoring of a letter asking for money overdue as insolence – as indeed it is. If a prompt reply is dispatched with a careful explanation of the difficulties and an indication of a payment date, much trouble (sometimes serious trouble) may be avoided.

Addressing Envelopes

Unless the contents of your letter are strictly personal or confidential, it is not wise to mark your envelope accordingly. Your correspondent may be away when your letter arrives, and your "personal" address may prevent the opening of the envelope by his or her deputy.

It is customary to add the words "Messrs" before all firms trading by name – for example, "Messrs A G Blank & Tomson" – but not before companies or firms trading under impersonal titles – for example, The Cloud Formation Company Limited. One should not really abbreviate the names of addressees; for instance, if the firm is Messrs Alfred Canford Johnson & Company, it is safer not to write to them as Messrs A C Johnson & Company, or your letter may be delivered to the wrong firm.

For male individuals, "Mr" followed by the name is used, unless there is any other title. Formerly "Esq" was used for men who owned land but nowadays "Mr" has been adopted as the general rule. "Mr" can also be used when the person's initials are unknown, but in this case, when writing to an individual in a firm, it is more polite to send the letter addressed to the firm, marked for attention, thus:

FIELD & FIELD LIMITED
253 High Street, Lincoln, LN1 7YY

2 November XXXX

For the attention of Mr Binks
Smith & Smith Limited
21 North Road
Epsom
Surrey
KT1 5TT

Dear Sirs

If you are writing to a woman and you know her marital status, then address her as "Miss" or "Mrs" accordingly. But if you don't know whether she is married or not, or if you know she prefers the title "Ms", use that instead.

Addressing an Envelope to a UK Address

When addressing an envelope to someone in the UK, always try to put the postcode on a line on its own, and to make it the last line of the address. It must be clearly printed in capitals, with no punctuation, and it should not be underlined. Leave a small gap between the two halves of the code. If you do not have enough space to put the postcode on its own line, it is acceptable to put it alongside the county name, leaving a space of about 2cm between them. It is worth noting that if you are writing to the United Kingdom from abroad, the postcode should still be the last line of the address.

It is also preferable to put the main postal town, which must be written clearly in capitals, on its own line.

Where possible, you should try to include the name of the county, particularly if you are sending something to a town which has the same name as others located in different counties – like Ashford or Newport.

If your letter is going to someone who lives in a country village which has a larger post town, it is not necessary to put the words “Near” or “By” before the name of the post town. Nor should you put the word “Local” if the letter is going to someone in your own area.

Here are two examples of how to write the types of addresses mentioned. On the left is a *fully blocked* (aligned) style with *open punctuation* (i.e. not punctuated) suitable for a typewritten letter. On the right, is a handwritten address, fully punctuated and indented, sent from overseas.

Mrs Geraldine Steele
12 Viking Avenue
Wishingbury
BRISTOL
Avon BS7 5PZ

Mr. P. Jones,
 8, The Grove,
  ST. ALBANS,
   Herts.
    UNITED KINGDOM
     AL10 9PP

The name and address of the recipient should be placed in the *bottom* half of the front of the envelope, slightly to the left-hand side. One simple reason for this is that if you write the address too high up, you may not have enough room for the stamp(s). (How many of us have written the address too high on our small Christmas card envelopes, only to find that the name is partially covered by a lovely big Christmas stamp!) Another reason is that the name and/or address could become obliterated by the postmark if it is written too high up.

If you are writing to someone you think may have moved, it is a good idea to put the words “Please Forward” on the front of the envelope, in the top left-hand corner, and to write on the flap on the reverse of the envelope, “If undelivered, please return to”, then your name and address. This saves either the current occupants (who may not have a forwarding address), or the Post Office, opening your private mail to find out to whom they should return the letter. For the same reason, it is also sensible to include your address on the back of the envelope if you write to someone with whom you have not corresponded for a long time.

Addressing an Envelope to an Overseas Address

Much of the advice above also applies here, and again, you should always write the address in the bottom half of the front of the envelope, slightly to the left.

Any air mail stickers or other service instructions should be placed or written on the front of the envelope in the top left-hand corner. As a general rule when writing overseas, I would always put on the reverse outside flap of the envelope "If undelivered please return to", followed by my name and address. Again, it saves having personal mail opened if it cannot be delivered for any reason.

Other countries have their own coding systems (called 'zip' codes in many places, such as the USA and Australia), which are similar to our postcodes, and these need to be clearly marked. However, when writing overseas from the United Kingdom, you should make the country of destination the last line of the address. Imagine how frustrating it would be if a letter bound for Kingston, Jamaica ended up in Kingston, Surrey!

Sending Your Letters

There are many ways in which you can send your mail within the UK and to overseas destinations, and it is not really possible to give details of them all in a book of this kind.

Apart from the obvious first and second class postal services, some others available are: Recorded, Registered and Special Delivery; International Registered Delivery; and Swiftair services. It is worth bearing in mind that all these services will cost you – to a greater or lesser degree – more than if you sent your item by ordinary first class post; and that hardly anything is so annoying as to receive a letter by one of these means which contains information of little or no importance or urgency.

There is obviously a great deal to know about the various postal services available, and for more information I would suggest you ask at your local post office for a leaflet, or consult *The Post Office Guide*, a copy of which should be in the reference section of your local library.

Stamping Your Mail

The correct place for a stamp is on the front of the envelope in the top right-hand corner. If possible, use only one stamp of the correct value. However, if you have to use more than one stamp, they should be placed side by side. Do not cover stamps with sticky tape as the Post Office need to be able to cancel them.

3
Grammar and Punctuation

This chapter is the briefest of introductions to the immense subject of grammar and punctuation, and although it is better to try and get your grammar and punctuation correct in anything you write, remember that they are not the most important things in your letters.

What matters is what your letters say; and what they say results from the amount of thought and consideration that you have given to them.

This is particularly the case when writing to friends, who will be delighted that you have taken the trouble to write at all!

Write as if you are speaking your thoughts aloud; pack your letters with interesting news and information that your readers will enjoy. Worry more about the content of your letter than about the grammar or punctuation, and you will not go far wrong.

The ordinary businessman need not be unduly anxious about the way he expresses himself; he should certainly avoid becoming so conscious of his grammar (or lack of it) that he holds a *post mortem* on each sentence he writes. If his firm employs a secretary or shorthand typist, who can be relied upon to maintain the essentials of grammar, much can be left to her judgment. There are also numerous books of reference which are helpful.

The businessman should remember that his letters will not be carefully analysed and scrutinized by his correspondents – who, in any event, may be no better grammarians than he – *but they must be easily understood and they must not be ambiguous*. He must at all costs avoid writing a jumbled and illiterate letter which, apart from the general undesirability of bad writing, may have serious business consequences. Equally, however, he should not spend valuable time pondering over the use (or misuse) of a comma. Punctuation cannot make an illiterate letter literate, but it avoids ambiguity and clarifies the meaning which the construction of the sentences might not give without it.

It is the recording of *your* thoughts into well-chosen meaningful words with their harmonious flow (which you can check by reading aloud) rather than school teacher's grammar, which gives a letter power and impact.

Grammar

The trouble with grammar, as with punctuation, is that many people tend to worry too much about it. Grammar should be learned almost unconsciously. If you listen to and read well-spoken and written English, you will acquire the right habits and will rarely find yourself going wrong. However, there are a few rules which can be remembered as a guide.

Paragraphs

Paragraphing is not so much a matter of personal taste, rather it is used to divide a letter into subjects or definite parts of subjects. It is advisable to keep paragraphs reasonably short, if possible; one of more than fifteen lines becomes rather tedious to the reader, who is subconsciously, if not consciously, looking for a break in the continuous flow of text. Do not begin a fresh paragraph, however, to obey this maxim at the expense of continuity but wait until there is a suitable break in the subject matter. Sometimes a short paragraph is used for emphasis and it may (though normally it should not) consist of only one sentence. Do not, therefore, overdo this striving for effect or you may defeat your intention.

Sentences

When you are not quite sure whether a sentence is correctly written, it is a good plan to parse or split it into its component parts. This often exposes mistakes which you may otherwise miss. Take the following sentence: "Just as whisky serves a useful purpose, so should wine, but all too often neither do". Can you see anything wrong with that sentence? Write it out in full: Just as whisky serves a useful purpose, so should wine serve a useful purpose, but all too often neither the one nor the other *does*. It then becomes apparent where your mistake lies. Errors of case are all too frequent and they often pass unnoticed. You might reply to the question: "To whom does your business belong?" with the words: "To my partner, Mr Smith, and I". But you would not say, "To I". If, therefore, you implement your answer with the one word *to,* you can see your mistake immediately and will change the case of your pronoun, *I,* to the objective, *me.* In everyday speech, you will often hear the phrase, "Between you and I", but you will realise that, in your writing, you should use the grammatically accurate form, "Between you and (between) me".

Ask yourself what is wrong with the words "for you and I", and the answer is that it should be "for you and me". This you can prove by filling in the missing word "for", making the full phrase "for you and (for) me". You will then see that the first phrase "for you and I" could not be correct.

Length of Sentences

As to the length of his sentences, a wise motto for the beginner might be "Keep them short until you have sufficient command of the English language to lengthen them without sacrificing clarity." Most difficulties only arise when one tries to write sentences beyond one's grasp; one then gets lost in a tangle of confused thought and loose construction. Think out what you want to write before putting it down.

Common Errors

Always be sure that a sentence is complete; that is, complete with a subject (a noun or pronoun) and verb. Here is an example, "She went to the door to open it. But did not try." The first sentence is complete, the second is not because it has no subject. It should read, "But she did not try."

Here is an example of a sentence which is incomplete because the subject and verb have been omitted: "Standing on the pavement with the dog." If, before the word "standing", you put the words "I was", the sentence would be complete.

It is usually better not to end a sentence with a preposition. An example of this is the following sentence: "This is the letter which I've been waiting for." The sentence should read: "This is the letter for which I've been waiting."

"And" and "but" are words which should, as far as possible, be kept away from the beginnings of sentences. However, they are sometimes used there on purpose, for emphasis.

Another difficulty that arises is the use of "either... or" and "neither... nor". So often you read sentences such as this: "She looked, but he was neither in the garage or the garden." Here, confusion has led to the mixing of the positive and negative sentence. In this – the negative sentence – it should read: "She looked, but he was neither in the garage *nor* the garden."

The positive example would be as follows: "She thought he must be in either the garage or the garden."

Split Infinitives

A split infinitive is an adverb or adverbial phrase inserted between "to" and the verb. For example: "to quickly walk"; "to boldly go where no man has gone before". "To fully appreciate" is a split infinitive, but "to be fully appreciated" is not. That eminent authority on the correct use of the English language, H W Fowler, has summed up the position by saying that it is never advisable to split an infinitive with a long phrase and only to do so when ambiguity or awkwardness would otherwise arise. This gives reasonable scope to most writers.

It is a very common fault not least because, more often than not, it sounds more correct the *wrong* way than the right! Another example of a split infinitive is: "I would like you to urgently send your new catalogue." Here, "urgently" has been inserted between the sign of the infinitive, "to", and its verb, "send". The sentence should read: "I would like you to send urgently your new catalogue." OR: "I would like you urgently to send your new catalogue."

The rule here is never to split the word "to" from its verb.

Superlatives

The use of double superlatives for emphasis should be avoided. Sufficient emphasis can be obtained with such words as "very"; for example, "great big" is better as "very big" or "very large". "Great" and "big" have the same meaning, therefore "great big" is like saying "big big" – the kind of expression used by children or foreigners only slightly acquainted with the English language. Often, also the "very" is unnecessary if another word can be used; in our example, "enormous" might do. It's often more effective.

Open Punctuation

This refers to the omission of commas and full stops in the salutation, complimentary closing and addresses of your letters. It is common in typewritten material, especially business letters, because it saves time in the typing.

In handwritten letters, although many people leave out the comma at the end of each line of the address, it is still usual to put the full stop after "Mr./Mrs.", etc., and to include the comma after "Dear *name*,". In the same way, when you finish a handwritten letter, you would always include the comma after "Yours sincerely,".

Envelopes tend to follow the punctuation of the letter inside.

In this book, I have used open punctuation for business and official letters. Where a letter would obviously be a handwritten one, I have included commas and full stops where appropriate.

Punctuation

Punctuation has become a matter largely of individual taste, although there are certain fundamental points to remember. As with most subjects, the correct use of punctuation is a great bone of contention among experts. There are two extreme schools of thought – those who favour the academically correct and frequent use of punctuation, and those who insist upon the minimum. The rest of the world falls between these two extremes.

"Punctuation" is a word which frightens a great many people unnecessarily. Those who paid close attention to it at school may have no fears, but for the rest of us it is sometimes worrying. And that, I believe, is the worst feature of it; over-anxiety can lead us to make annoying little mistakes which we normally wouldn't make.

Most of us have a basic grasp of punctuation, but it is worth reminding ourselves of just what it means and when it should be used.

The first things to remember are, I think, the punctuation marks – the full stop, the comma, the semi-colon, the colon, the question mark, the exclamation mark, inverted commas, the apostrophe, the hyphen, brackets, and the dash.

Although this seems like a long list, many of these punctuation marks are not always used in general and social letter writing.

The Full Stop (.)

The first, most important and final mark is the full stop. If we say it can safely be used to divide sentences, or sentences and subordinate clauses, which are not closely related to one another, we shall not go far wrong. Too many full stops detract from the flow and rhythm of one's writing and produce a staccato effect, as does also an excess of exclamation marks(!).

The full stop is used where a definite break is necessary and where the sentence is complete. If no full stops were inserted in a piece of writing, it would be almost impossible to read. For examples, have a look at the sentences in this book.

The Comma (,)

Always think of the comma as the smallest stop. In other words, put it in where, if you were speaking, you would stop to breathe, or where there is a natural pause.

Many people think that a comma is unnecessary before the words "and" and "but". Generally this is true but in some instances a comma before these words can make the sentence clearer or more easily read.

If commas are left out, a sentence can read wrongly and might be misunderstood; however, for this very same reason many lawyers leave out all commas when drawing up legal documents!

Basically, commas are used at the ends of phrases or where you would pause to take a breath. Therefore, provided you don't insert one in the middle of a clause, you can't go wrong. The main thing to remember is to put them in your sentences when a slight break is required.

A comma provides the shortest break of all. As a rule it should be inserted between adjectives preceding and qualifying substantives – for instance: "An upright, haughty figure" – but not in cases where the last adjective is in closer relation to the substantive than to the preceding adjectives – for instance: "A famous foreign diplomat". It is also used to enclose interpolations, etc., in this way taking the place of parentheses (or brackets); in these cases the sentence should read quite well *without* the word or words between commas. It should strictly not be used where "and" joins two single words or phrases.

The following is an example to illustrate the misuse and use of the comma:

Karen and James have decided to go down to the coast for the weekend so they've booked their hotel checked the car and had a look at the map to find the best route.

Although it can be understood, see how much easier this sentence reads when it has a few commas in it:

Karen and James have decided to go down to the coast for the weekend, so they've booked their hotel, checked the car, and had a look at the map to find the best route.

The Semi-colon (;)
The semi-colon is used when you need a slightly longer pause than that which you would get with a comma. A semi-colon very often forms a substitute for a full stop, to avoid starting too many new sentences. Notice that the ideas after a semi-colon have to relate in some way to those immediately before it. Below is an example of how to use the semi-colon:

Karen and James enjoyed their trip to the coast at the weekend; the weather was beautiful and they spent much of their time water-skiing.

The grouping of several complete sentences which are *closely related in sense* can be divided by semi-colons and this generally makes for easier and more restful reading than the substitution of full stops. It also avoids the use of too many "ands" – a conjunction should not normally follow a semi-colon. For instance: "The remarks you made in your last letter can be more fully discussed at our next meeting; I shall not go further into the matter now.", shows the use of the semi-colon. This could have been divided into two sentences by using a full stop, but the semi-colon carries less finality and the flow of meaning is maintained without too great a break.

The Colon (:)
The colon is generally used before a list, or as an

indication that something is to follow, for example:

The following people were elected to the committee:

Natalie Hardwick
Sarah Hamilton
Simon Phillips
Richard Castleton.

The colon can be used before a quotation – for example: "In his reply, Mr Jones said: 'I am grateful to our chairman for having summed up the whole matter so simply and expertly'." (A comma could be used in place of a colon, where the sense is preserved.)

The Apostrophe (')

This can indicate that a letter has been left out of a word; for instance if you are changing "have not" to "haven't" it shows that the "o" has been omitted.

Many people are unsure of how to use the apostrophe with the word "it". The general rule is that if you can't substitute "it is", or "it has", when you read your sentence, it should be "its" (i.e. no apostrophe). For example, "the dog scratched its leg" (correct; you could not put in "it is"). However, if you say, "it's the only one we have", this would be correct because you could easily substitute "it is" in the place of "it's"; or "it's been raining today" (correct again; "it has" could be inserted).

The apostrophe is also used when denoting ownership, to make a shorter and better phrase as, for example, "the woman's coat", rather than "the coat of the woman", or "the man's hat", instead of "the hat of the man". When the apostrophe is used with plural words it comes *after* the "s". So if you wanted to talk about the socks of some boys or the dresses of several girls, you would refer to "the boys' socks" and "the girls' dresses". However when using a *collective* word (different from a plural word but which still suggests more than one person or thing), like "children" or "people", the apostrophe goes *before* the "s"; i.e. "the children's pony", or "the people's cars".

Note that the abbreviation is *not* used for inanimate objects; one never says "The table's leg" for "The leg of the table". As the apostrophe indicates a missing letter or letters, it is also used in such words as "aren't" to show that the "o" of "not" has been omitted. Be careful that it does, in fact, show the position of the missing letter – not "are'nt", as is sometimes seen. As a matter of interest in this connection, the phrase "The boy's pencil" really stands for "The boy his pencil", the "hi" being replaced by an apostrophe to make it less clumsy.

An emerging practice, roundly to be deplored, is the use of what I would term the "intrusive" apostrophe. The misuse is seen where an apostrophe is inserted into an ordinary plural word. Once limited to greengrocers' signs (banana's, avocado's, etc.) it is now spreading to other shops (video's – two for the price of one) and is even seen in newspaper advertisements (two secretary's needed)(!). The commonest pitfall is in the word "its" (as in for its own sake), often mis-spelt "it's". But remember "it's" is short for it is (as in "it's a knockout").

A final warning: in writing, the apostrophe should only be used in the possessive case, it creates a bad impression to use it for lazy abbreviations such as "aren't" and "didn't", except in personal letters. Normally, use "did not" etc.

The Exclamation Mark (!)

This is mainly used to express surprise, emphasis, sarcasm or humour, as in the following examples:

The cat's had *eight* kittens!
Peter told the dog to STAY!
Why on earth did you think I'd want *that*!
We're having a new bathroom put in, so the place is like a building site at the moment!

An exclamation mark follows an interjection – Alas! Hello!, etc. It often underlies sarcasm, for example: "I like the English weather!" When following a quotation, as a *comment* by the person quoting, it should be outside the inverted commas, thus: He said "All men are liars"! In such a case it indicates disagreement with the quotation.

The Question Mark (?)

This follows a direct question where an answer is required, as well as a rhetorical question, which is a statement in the form of a question. Examples of this are: "May I come in?" (Direct); "What sort of a remark do you call *that?*" (Rhetorical: used for effect.)

There should be no difficulty over the use of question and exclamation marks, provided you do not confuse the two. Be careful to make sure that your question *is* a question and not a statement of fact or opinion. For instance: "Can you arrange to meet me at 5.30 p.m. on Tuesday next?" is correct, but "I wonder if I could see the manager" can be written without a question mark.

Brackets ( )

These are used where something is put into a sentence, usually to clarify the meaning, but which has no direct effect on the sense of the sentence. For example: "The boys (there were four of them) stood at the bus stop."

Alternatively, commas could be used in the place of the brackets.

Dashes can also be used in the place of brackets. In business correspondence dashes and brackets may seldom be necessary, and should be avoided wherever possible unless the writer is confident that he will use them correctly. For example: "Thank you for your letter – and what a nice letter it is!"; "I have enclosed a cheque for £200 (two hundred pounds)." Dashes and brackets are often used for similar purposes, such as clarification, explanation, etc., when it is felt they will make easier reading than with commas. Examples: "The books, new and old, were on the table", or "The books (new and old) were on the table" or "The books – new and old – were on the table". It will be seen that in this example, commas, brackets and dashes all serve the same purpose.

Inverted Commas (“ ”)
These are often referred to as quotes. They are generally used to enclose an extract or quotation, or when recalling what someone has said. For example:

“If music be the food of love, play on.”
(Quotation from *Twelfth Night* by William Shakespeare.)
“The football’s started,” shouted Paul.

They are used also to point a metaphor, thus: “Life’s fitful fever”. They are often found misused in addresses when enclosing the name of a house. Use them when the name is a *quotation,* thus, “Clovelly”, but not “Cobblestones”. See also page 132.

The Hyphen (-)
The hyphen is self-explanatory; common sense will help you to use it correctly. More and more, today, it is being omitted from common words, as for example “book-seller” is more often written “bookseller” (this form has a foreign flavour), or “book seller”. The first is strictly correct; the latter rarely seen.

The hyphen can be used when two words would read better as one, as in:

brightly-coloured
flip-flops
second-hand
dimly-lit.

The Dash (–)
When printed, dashes are usually longer than hyphens; and these two punctuation marks have quite different meanings.

Dashes are often used instead of commas or semi-colons. The best explanation of a dash is to give a couple of examples.

The couple – still covered in confetti – went off on honeymoon.

Sorry I’ve taken so long to reply – I can’t believe it’s October already!

4
The Risks of Letter Writing

The dangers of the written word in social letters are mainly more of a social nature than of a legal one. There is no question that letters can be the cause of family squabbles and of serious differences, sometimes tragic, between friends, purely owing to hasty action or misunderstandings.

The message of this chapter is to advise the reader to be extremely careful in writing anything of a dangerous character, and to be careful that the phrasing of the letter is such that it cannot be misunderstood.

Letters should not be written in the heat of the moment, or, if they are, they should be laid aside and considered the next day. When something disagreeable has to be said to someone, or about someone, it is very much safer to do so verbally and in confidence.

It must be realised that between close friends much more can be written than could be sent to comparative strangers. It is largely a question of knowing to whom you are writing, but the need for care is always present. Think twice before you write once.

A 'Threatening' Letter

Another potential danger is that some people may, in the heat of the moment, make a written threat without realising the possible legal consequences. The law takes an extremely serious view of anything of this nature. For example, someone in a fit of anger may write:

If you don't stop parking your car across my driveway, I'll smash it to bits and dump it in your front garden.

As you can imagine, it is extremely unwise to write anything of this kind, where you are basically saying that you will take the law into your own hands. There are legal processes which exist to resolve such situations.

If such a letter has to be sent, it could be written in a legal way, for example:

Private and Confidential (envelope the same)

For several days now you have been parking your car across my driveway so that I am unable to get into my garage. As I am sure you would not want me to refer the matter to my solicitor, will you please stop doing this immediately.

So long as you were sure, and had some evidence of the problem, there could be no danger in sending such a letter; although, depending on the seriousness of the situation, you may not need to mention your solicitor.

Receiving A Threatening Letter

If you receive a written threat that has obviously been written purely in the heat of the moment, probably your best solution would be just to ignore it.

However, if you receive a *serious* written threat you should consult a solicitor, or put the matter into the hands of the police. The difficulty of the latter procedure is that the police might insist on taking some action, against your wishes; whereas, normally, a solicitor will be guided by your instructions.

Blackmail

Blackmail is where money or some service is demanded under threat of exposure. It doesn't matter whether the information the sender threatens to expose is true or false; the law takes a very grave view of the blackmailer.

We are always seeing reports in the Press where prominent figures have been the subject of blackmail threats when their letters have fallen into the hands of unauthorised (and unscrupulous) people. This illustrates only too clearly how careful we should all be when writing anything of a confidential nature.

Chain Letters

At some time in our lives, almost every one of us will receive a chain letter. The concept behind them is to perpetuate the chain, by the recipient sending copies of the letter to others. Many also involve the sending of money.

Chain letters will normally be sent to you by someone you know. However, it is unlikely that you will know who originated the letter, as such letters can be in existence for many months, or even years.

Some chain letters can contain veiled threats, or are designed to intimidate the recipient into continuing the chain. These, however, seem to be few and far between, and most chain letters are no more than a nuisance.

What to do with them is up to you, but personally, I always throw any chain letters straight in the bin!

Pen Friends

Thousands of people make use of pen friend clubs which can be found all over the world. In many cases, it is a way of making new friends from different countries and cultures. In most instances, the resulting friendships are innocent and genuine, and many pen friends, who may have been corresponding for years, do get the chance to meet.

There is, however, a danger that pen friend clubs could be joined by ill-intentioned people for unpleasant or perverted reasons, and one must always be aware of this fact if making arrangements to meet a pen friend – however long you have been writing to them.

Copyright

Another pitfall which you could encounter (and of which you may not be aware) when you write is breach of copyright.

Whenever anything is spoken or written, it automatically becomes copyright. Even in a private letter one must not quote others without permission and acknowledgement of the source. That is the legal position but, of course, if you are quoting in a letter what your wife said when she sat on a pin...

Well, that's different!

Again, it is normal practice to quote brief extracts, using inverted commas, from various printed sources, provided you are using them to explain some point, or confirm some view you hold. Give the source of the extract, especially if it is a long one.

Quoting from another source in a personal letter is quite different from doing so in material which is going to be published for the public. This cannot be done safely without permission. A good example of this type of letter would be one to The Editor of a newspaper, where permission to publish is taken as being granted.

The copyright of a letter belongs to the writer of it; if A writes you a letter, you are not entitled to take extracts from it to pass on to B or with a view to any form of publicity without A's permission. If A had made libellous or defamatory remarks in his letter, you would be extremely unwise to pass them on and might find yourself in legal trouble.

Describing Goods for Sale

Care must also be taken, when describing goods, not to contravene the Trade Descriptions Act.

Libel, Slander and Defamation of Character

The wit who said, "Do right and fear no man; don't write and fear no woman", exaggerated. However, it is true that many letters are written which in law undoubtedly provide grounds for libel, defamation of character or even breach of promise but of which, for a variety of reasons, nothing more is heard.

The word "libel" means any malicious or defamatory piece of writing, art, recording or broadcast, and must be avoided at all costs, unless done under privilege. ("Slander" has basically the same meaning, but applies to the spoken word.)

It is also widely believed that the truth is not libellous nor slanderous, but this is not necessarily so. Indeed, the truth can possibly be more dangerous than fiction.

Let us imagine that my next door neighbour had assaulted somebody twenty years ago and had received a term of imprisonment; in other words he had committed a crime and paid the legal penalty. It would be the truth if I should inform others in the neighbourhood that this man who had recently become my neighbour was an ex-convict, but you can see how unfair it would be to him, because the conviction was so long ago that it is "spent". He could, in my opinion rightly, take action against me.

Libel, being written, is more punishable in law than slander, because of the permanency of the written word.

The letter beginning "I am writing to tell you what I think of you", and continuing to inform the recipient what you think of him, can be libellous. Although addressed to the individual and not "published", the fact that it has been written and sent is in itself publication. However, there are instances where statements can be made quite legally, if done in the proper manner.

Perhaps the most common example is a reference as to character or integrity; if something disparaging has to be said, provided it is done in good faith and without malice, and what is said is true and headed "Private and Confidential", much can be written which would otherwise be actionable. It is, of course, essential for the envelope containing the information to be properly sealed and also marked "Private and Confidential", and carefully addressed to the correct recipient.

The libel position is hedged about with so many technicalities that only an expert can give an opinion on any particular case – and even the opinion of an expert might be proved wrong in a Court of Law. On the other hand, a great deal of privilege is allowed, provided precautions are taken. Equally, custom and some knowledge of the person to whom you are writing play their parts in such matters. One sensible precaution is that the originator should himself put any important letter into its envelope, after reading and signing it, to ensure that no mistakes are made.

In the ordinary course of business many situations arise which call for strong wording; I give below some examples of letters which are perfectly "safe", provided the letter is addressed personally to a director or senior official of the firm concerned and that the words "Private and Confidential" appear on the envelope and directly above the recipient's name on the letter itself. Always remember, however, that if in any doubt, be *very careful* what you write.

Imagine, for example, that I have bought one hundred leather wallets from a representative. On delivery, I discover they are not leather but are made of imitation skin. I have nothing in writing, but wish to get the correct position established at the earliest moment.

Dear Mr Baxter

A week ago your representative called here and sold me one hundred leather wallets at £50 each. On delivery, I found that these wallets are made of some imitation skin, and I am accordingly writing to inform you I cannot accept these at the price you charge, i.e., £50 each. In my view, a reasonable price for these imitation leather articles would be £15 each, and if you are not prepared to reduce them accordingly, I propose to return the consignment.

I await your reply.

Yours sincerely
PARKER & PARKER

D E Parker

This letter contains an implicit accusation, but there is nothing dangerous about it as it is addressed personally to the head of the firm concerned, who should open it so that it cannot get into the hands of any other members of the staff – an eventuality which might affect the situation.

A second example is:

Dear Mr Fullsome

I have just heard you are offering our 5cm oak planks, bearing our brand, as being two years dry. If you will refer to our quotation and confirmation of order, you will find that the planks were sold to you as one year dry.

This letter is to request you to alter your offers to conform with the terms under which the goods were sold, as we cannot allow our brand to be misrepresented.

An acknowledgement of this letter, and your agreement to the suggested course of action, will be appreciated.

Yours sincerely
SMITH & JONES LIMITED

G H Smith
Director

The following letters constitute correspondence between Blandish & Owen Limited and the Writa Pen Company Limited:

Dear Mr Stanford-Brown

A very serious matter has arisen in connection with the delivery of 1,000 fountain pens against our order number 0783.

We regret to inform you that these pens have proved extremely unsatisfactory. Frequent complaints have been received from our customers to the effect that the pens leak and will not write without blotting. Quite frankly, they fall considerably below our usual standard and we think the best way out of the difficulty will be for you to authorise the return of the balance of the consignment, which is 937 pens.

The functioning of the pens has been compared with the sample left by your representative, and in our view the bulk of the shipment contains defects and is inferior to the sample.

Your comments will be appreciated.

Yours sincerely
BLANDISH & OWEN LIMITED

K C Blandish

Dear Mr Blandish

In reply to your letter of 2 July XXXX, we would point out that all our pens are manufactured to be, and to the best of our knowledge are, identical in design and performance. In any case, as you have accepted delivery and broken bulk, we cannot accept the return of the goods or entertain any claim.

Yours sincerely
THE WRITA PEN COMPANY LIMITED

G Stanford-Brown
Sales Manager

Dear Mr Stanford-Brown

We are surprised at the attitude adopted in your letter of 4 July XXXX. In view of the fact that the pens are manufactured articles we do not believe that bulk being broken has any bearing on the case as the flaws were not visible. Before taking further action, do you not think it would be wise to send a representative to inspect the goods?

Yours sincerely
BLANDISH & OWEN LIMITED

K C Blandish

A dangerous reply would be one which inferred that you intended telling the whole trade of the treatment received from the Writa Pen Company. That might provoke legal action for malicious defamation of character. Although the firm had admittedly behaved badly, they might be legally within their rights. On the other hand, it is customary to warn your friends against trading with such a concern, provided the warning is given verbally to people under whose discretion you can depend.

Should the firm in question be a member of any trade association, it is often worthwhile to advise them you intend to put the matter before their association unless they adopt a more reasonable attitude; many firms will be prepared to reach some amicable agreement rather than jeopardise their reputation. It *rarely* pays to go to law, but in certain instances it is wise to get a solicitor's opinion and consider it.

Among other matters that may arise are letters with insurance companies, where you have a genuine complaint. Let us imagine that the insurance company, after negotiation, has declined to pay you £xxxx for damages to which you feel entitled, and that their offer has been £xxx. A suitable reply is:

Dear Sirs

With reference to your letter of 17 October XXXX, I cannot accept the £xxx offered, and must insist on the full £xxxx compensation to which I feel entitled. This is the lowest figure I am prepared to accept, and unless this matter is settled to my satisfaction within fourteen days I shall regretfully be obliged to issue a writ.

Yours faithfully

This rather strong line will usually achieve results because large companies dislike going to law unless they are sure they have a good case. The same remarks apply to any other similar instances. If you take a strong line you will nearly always win your point, *provided you are in the right*.

The following is an example of a libellous letter:

Dear Sirs

Your representative called here yesterday and offered a representative of our firm a £xxx bribe to take no action over the question of the inferior quality of your recent delivery of barrels.

We hereby notify you that we are closing your account and you may inform your representative that he will not be required to come here again; in fact it would be wiser for him not to do so.

Yours faithfully

C Thomas

Even though it may be true that the representative offered some form of bribe, it would obviously be extremely difficult to prove; in putting your accusation in writing you would immediately expose yourself to a very serious risk – defamation of character. The latter part of the letter also contains a hidden threat, and threatening letters are particularly dangerous.

Letters Asking for Payment

Terms for payment vary in different trades, but in them all there will be good payers, slow payers and those who never intend to pay at all. Slow payers must be treated with care. It is an unfortunate human weakness that most of us are gravely offended when asked for money. Many firms have lost accounts which might have developed into good propositions because the accountant, cashier, representative, or even the Managing Director has written a tactless letter regarding some outstanding account.

It is best to treat each customer as an individual, and if an account has been rendered more than once it is customary to add to it the words "Kindly remit", while if it has been rendered two or three times some stronger request can be made – for example, "As this account is now three months overdue, please remit within seven days".

On the other hand, many firms prefer to include a letter with the account asking for payment. It is wise to take the greatest care in such a matter or much valuable goodwill may be sacrificed. If the letter is worded diplomatically, the recipient is less liable to be offended. Remember always to address your letter to a senior official of the firm concerned and to include the words "Private and Confidential" on both the envelope and the letter.

You could send a letter similar to this one:

Dear Mr Whiteway

We enclose our account for £550.45, which is now two months overdue. We feel you may have overlooked this, and shall be glad of a remittance as soon as possible.

Yours sincerely

G Case
Manager

If the debtor ignores your request, sterner measures must be taken:

Dear Mr Whiteway

Your account is now three months overdue and you will appreciate that we cannot run our business unless we receive payment for goods delivered.

We shall be glad if you will make payment by return, or let us have some suggestion as to how and when you will pay so that we may consider it.

Yours sincerely

G Case
Manager

N.B. This type of letter should be sent by Recorded Delivery.

It is often better not to write but to call in person. Sometimes you might have to accept a part payment in full settlement.

With *dishonest* people, firm handling and the threat of a writ may produce the desired result.

It may have been obvious that I have avoided any suggestion of actually putting an unpaid account into the hands of a lawyer. Many people who do not pay accounts are also not deterred by solicitors; they know they can delay any legal action for some weeks by an exchange of correspondence – all of which will cost you money. In fact, in the UK, it is not worth instructing solicitors to issue a writ unless the amount of money is substantial. For smaller amounts, a debt-collecting company can be used (these generally charge a percentage of money recovered), but this will often not succeed if you have already done everything possible yourself.

Issuing Writs

Do not lightly issue a writ unless you mean it and believe it to be worthwhile. If you do, issue it after having given due notice. The warning, however, will often prove to be sufficient. If you issue the writ instead of employing a legal firm to do it, it will be cheaper and probably just as effective. If you prefer to work through a lawyer, do not allow him to procrastinate unduly; ask him to send a short note requesting payment or threatening a writ. If no reply is received, *instruct* your solicitor to attend to the writ. What you must avoid is to allow the lawyer to send his clerk, write several letters, make phone calls, etc., or you may find that even if he gets the money in the end much of it has been dissipated by his expenses and costs.

A stronger demand might be worded as follows:

Dear Sir

We are writing to request payment of our account, which has remained overdue for three months.

Unless payment is received within seven days we regret we have no alternative but to issue a writ without further notice.

Yours faithfully

G Case
Manager

The following kind of legal approach can be very successful:

PRIVATE AND CONFIDENTIAL

TO: (Name)
OF: (Address)

SUM DUE: (Amount in words)

BE ADVISED Papers are in preparation for legal proceedings to be taken against you in your nearest Court to recover the sum of £xxx when application will also be made to that Court for an Order to charge the total costs of this Action against you.

IF you wish to avoid such Action by payment of the amount due, urgently send it to this address to arrive not later than (date – allow ten days, making sure it will not occur during a weekend; if so, go on to the Monday).

DATED (Date in words)
SIGNED (Signature)

Part 2
Official Letters

5
Starting an Official Letter

The term "official" in this chapter refers to all letters that are not of a social nature, and would usually mean a letter written to a business or institution, or on behalf of an official body. The content and construction of such letters is normally quite different from social or business correspondence, which is why they are dealt with separately in this book.

There are many different businesses to which you may write – for example, your bank or building society, the electricity, gas, and telephone companies, or to your solicitor. You may also write letters on behalf of a local group, or contact a mail-order company requesting their latest catalogue. You might send letters to charities, the local council or to your MP. The list is endless. Nevertheless, the layout is basically the same for all official letters.

Presentation

It is most important that these letters can be easily read and understood. I always try to type any official letters, as I feel they look more professional, but it is perfectly acceptable to hand-write them. However, when doing so, your handwriting should be as neat as possible. You can imagine the headaches it could cause if information in a letter of this kind were to be misread.

It is vital that your name and address are clearly written, particularly if you are expecting a reply from someone who doesn't know you or your address. A good example of this is when sending away for something by mail order.

You know what your name is and where you live, but it can be a real puzzle for the company concerned when they try to work out where and to whom they should send the goods!

Setting out your Official Letters

The first things you should put on the letter are your address, the recipient's address, and the date. If you do not want to go to the expense of printed notepaper, it is quite adequate to write neatly your full address at the top of the paper.

Advising you to put your address on a letter may seem obvious, but it is surprising how many people write away for goods and do not include a return address!

There is no real necessity to include your name at the top with the address, as it will be written at the bottom along with your signature. I would normally include my telephone number but many people leave it out of the printed part and only write it in if they need an urgent response to the letter.

On any official correspondence, you should always include the full name and address of the recipient. The reason is that, as it will appear on your copy of the letter (see Keeping Copies of Correspondence, page 76), you will then have an address (and usually a name) reference in case of further correspondence.

It is most important to put the date on all official letters as it could make quite a difference, for instance when renewing insurance. A dated letter is also useful if you are expecting a reply, as you can see at a glance how long it is since you sent the letter.

The following example is the way in which I normally begin my official letters. I place my address at the right-hand margin, with the date below this. I then start writing/typing my recipient's name and address at the left-hand margin on or just below the same line as the date.

27 Cherry Way
HORSHAM
East Sussex
RH14 4BT

Mr James Williams *(the date)*
James Williams & Co Ltd
10 Eastfield Street
NEWCASTLE-UPON-TYNE
Tyne & Wear
NE6 7HY

The paragraphs of my letter are *blocked* at the left-hand margin, i.e. they are not indented. Instead, I leave an extra line space between them. You will notice that there is no punctuation in either of the addresses, nor would there be in the date, the "Dear Sir", or the "Yours faithfully". As explained earlier, this is described as *open punctuation*. There would, of course, be punctuation in the body of the letter itself!

Note here, that the main postal towns are in capitals, and they should always be on their own lines, if possible, as should the postcodes. It is also useful to include the county name in any address, as you will not always be writing to people from your own locality who know where your town is situated.

If you wished, you could use the *fully blocked* style. With this, you block *everything* at the left-hand margin, including your own address and the date, as in the following:

(your address)

(the date)

(recipient's address)

This second way is a very simple way to set out a letter, but it does take up a lot of space on the page.

You can also place your address and date information at the top, in the centre, but I don't feel that this works very well for letters to businesses and I, personally, would only use this style of layout when writing a letter to a friend (see Social Letters).

Opening and Closing

These are the "Dear..." and "Yours..." parts of your letter. The first of these is the 'opening', and is technically known as the *salutation*. The correct name for the 'closing' line is the *complimentary closing*.

There are really only two basic ways to start and end a letter to a business, so it couldn't be more simple. When writing to a named individual, you finish "Yours sincerely"; when you don't know a specific name, the letter should end "Yours faithfully". The following are the opening and closing lines which would therefore be used in the same letter.

Opening	*Closing*
Dear Sir(s), or, Dear Madam	Yours faithfully
Dear Mr/Mrs/Miss/Ms Smith, or, Dear John	Yours sincerely

If starting a letter with "Dear John" you could end with *Yours truly,* though I feel that this is a little outdated now.

When writing to a company (rather than to an office holder at the company), you would start *Dear Sirs,* or perhaps *Dear Sir or Madam* and close with *Yours faithfully.*

Many people nowdays often add an extra line before the

“Yours sincerely”, and this is usually something like *With kindest regards,* or *With very best wishes.* I would only add the latter if I knew quite well the person to whom I was writing.

Contact Names

Letters to businesses are now generally much more informal than they used to be. However, there is a danger that if you become too familiar too soon, it could be difficult if you then have to write a more formal letter (of complaint, perhaps) which really ought to begin “Dear Sir”.

That said, I still prefer to address my letters to a specific contact ‘name’. The most important reason for doing so is that you are, in my opinion, more likely to receive a reply. If you don’t, or something goes wrong, you always have someone with whom you can get in touch.

A contact name, or even a department name, is particularly useful when corresponding with big organisations where, if you write a general “Dear Sir” letter, it can get passed from department to department never to be seen again!

I would add here, that there is often an interminable delay when waiting for a reply from large organisations and you frequently have to be very patient! However, it is essential that you are persistent because some businesses (apart from their obvious inefficiency) may use ‘delaying tactics’ in the hope that you will become tired and abandon your correspondence. Keep on writing and referring to previous letters, and the fact that you have still not had a satisfactory reply, etc. And do not give up – however long it takes!

For The Attention Of...

Technically, there are two different ways to start a letter when writing to someone in particular at a company. The first is:

10 Beeches Road
LONDON
SW13 5UB

Mr Peter Hardwick *(the date)*
Green Fingers Garden Supplies
12 The Clears
TONBRIDGE
Kent
TN20 6XY

Dear Mr Hardwick

(You would close with "Yours sincerely".)

If you are writing a letter *For The Attention Of* a specific person at a company, you should set your letter out as follows:

10 Beeches Road
LONDON
SW13 5UB

Mr Peter Hardwick *(the date)*
Green Fingers Garden Supplies
12 The Clears
TONBRIDGE
Kent
TN20 6XY

Dear Sirs

For the attention of: Mr Peter Hardwick

(You would sign yourself "Yours faithfully".)

When addressing an envelope for either of these two letters, the Post Office require any "For the attention of..." information to be placed either *above* the address or to the left of it. It should not be put beneath the last line of the address. Thus you would put "Mr Peter Hardwick" or "For the attention of Mr Peter Hardwick" above the address.

Numbering Your Pages

If you are writing a letter of more than one page, you should always start each page on a fresh piece of paper; never use the back of the page. (This rule need not apply when writing social letters. See Starting a Social Letter, page 135.) There is no need to number the first page as it will be obvious from the address information at the top that this is where the letter begins. The top of each subsequent sheet may be set out like this:

Mr James Williams – 2 – *(the date)*
Williams & Co Ltd

The reason for putting the name (and company, if appropriate) of the recipient, with the date, is that if your pages become separated both you and the recipient will know to whom and when the information refers.

In addition to this heading on your continuation pages, you could also put a small prompt at the bottom of each page where there is a page to come after it. For example, at the bottom of page 1 you could put:

2/...

this would indicate to the reader that there is another page to follow.

When you have finished, it is always wise to staple the pages together, as this way they are less likely to become separated.

Signing Off

All letters should be hand-signed. You should also type

your name, or write it clearly in capitals, in addition to your signature. This is even more important if your signature is difficult to read, or, as in many cases, illegible!

Keeping Copies Of Correspondence

It is very important to keep copies of official letters (a complaint letter, or a letter to the bank, for example), as these may be needed in the future as proof of action or decision. They also serve you as excellent memory aids.

One method of keeping copies is by using carbon paper, and the type you can buy today is not nearly as messy as it used to be! Use flimsy paper for your copies; it is cheaper than the better quality paper you would use for actual letters.

A very useful product for doing copies is self-carboning copy paper which, as its name suggests, needs no carbon paper. It is generally available from good stationery shops.

Another way to keep copies is to photocopy your finished letters. If you do not have direct access to a copier, many libraries, high street stationers and print shops have a photocopying service available for a small charge.

Conclusion

The information above is designed to give you the basic guidelines for setting out and beginning your official letters.

The main points to remember are that these letters should contain all the relevant facts and information. They must be able to reach the correct person and be acted upon, and you must have good copies for your own future reference.

6

Simple Official Letters

In this chapter I have included a selection of simple letters covering a wide range of fairly common situations. I have shown a typewritten layout with *open punctuation.*

Quote for Flooring

This is a very simple letter to a company, requesting a quote for floor covering.

Dear Mr Henderson

Further to our visit to your showroom on Saturday, my wife and I have now decided on the hardwood parquet flooring and would like you to give us a quote to have the work done.

Our room measures approximately 5 metres by 4 metres but it would obviously be better if you could call round to measure up and to see exactly what the size is.

We will be at home any afternoon next week, so would look forward to seeing you then. Perhaps you could give us a call on the day to let us know what time you expect to arrive.

Yours sincerely

Bank Standing Order

A very common letter is one to your bank requesting the setting up of a standing order facility. This letter would normally be sent to "The Manager" who would then pass it on to the appropriate department.

Dear Sir

I would be grateful if you could arrange for a standing order of £20 to be transferred from my current account, number 23657987, to my building society savings account. The money should be transferred to:

Account Name	:	Stephen J Arrowsmith
Account No.	:	31416898
Building Society	:	The Hanover Building Society 10 Bridge Street MANCHESTER M3 8DX
Sort Code	:	00–36–69

Could transfers please be made on the first working day of every month, beginning in (*month*) and continuing until further notice.

I thank you in anticipation.

Yours faithfully

It is obviously important that when giving such instructions, you put the date on your letter; you should really date *ALL* your letters as advised in the previous chapter.

School – Child Ill

At some time, most parents will be required to write to their child's school teacher to advise of their child's illness. The following is an example of such a letter:

Dear Miss Blackwell,

I am writing to let you know that Tim will be unable to attend school this week as he has chicken-pox.

We had to call the doctor out to him on Friday evening as he was poorly and had started to develop spots. The doctor has said that we must keep him in isolation for seven days; so I would therefore expect him to be back at school next Monday or Tuesday.

With best wishes.

Yours sincerely,

Thanks for a Service Rendered

Although a high standard of service should be given by any company, it is unfortunate that this is not always the case. It is therefore a nice thought to write to someone when you have received particularly good service. Such a letter follows.

Dear Mr Dickens

I just wanted to send a note to say how very much my wife and I appreciate all the trouble you have gone to on our behalf to get the Texturelux wallpaper.

As you know, we had been all over the place trying to get this paper and it was not until we came into your shop that we received any sort of service. All too often nowadays, people are ready to criticise and complain, but can never be bothered to send a letter of praise and thanks when they receive the kind of excellent service such as my wife and I have from you. I am therefore sending a copy of this letter to your managing director so that he is aware of what a dedicated and willing salesman he has working in his company.

Once again, our grateful thanks.

Yours sincerely

Sending for Goods by Mail Order

Nowadays, many of us buy goods by mail order which we may have seen advertised in magazines or catalogues. An example of a letter requesting such goods is given below.

Dear Sirs

I was interested to read your advertisement in this week's *Woman's Realm*, and would be most grateful if you could send me a king-size duvet set in "Peaches and Cream", as mentioned. Enclosed is a cheque for the required amount.

Could you also please let me have your latest brochure and price list (including any postage charges) showing your complete range of curtains and soft furnishings in this design, as I think it is lovely and would like to co-ordinate my room around it.

I look forward to hearing from you.

Yours faithfully

Advising Businesses when you Move House

If you are moving house there are many businesses and institutions who will need to know your new address, for example, the bank, building society, any clubs or societies to which you may belong, etc. To save you time, you could just type out one letter on your present headed paper and have it photocopied. Such a letter could be based on the following:

Dear Sirs

Ref: *(any account number; membership number, etc.)*

I am writing to advise you that I am moving home. From the 12th of *month*, my new address will be:

4 Glovers Road
PETERBOROUGH
Cambs
PE4 8BU

Could you please amend your records accordingly.

Yours faithfully

Once you have photocopied your "master" copy, you can then fill in the relevant information, where necessary, on the photocopies.

Requesting Overdraft from Bank

This letter would be addressed to the manager, either by name if you know it, or by title.

Dear Sir *(or Dear Mr Briggs)*

You may be aware that in the last couple of weeks my account has had less money in it than usual, and I am writing to ask if I may have an overdraft facility of £200.

My reason for this request is that I have just had to pay out for my car insurance and it was a little more than I anticipated.

As you know, my salary is paid directly into my account on the 30th of each month, so funds will be paid in on a regular basis, and I would expect this overdraft to be cleared by the end of next month.

I do hope you will be able to send me a favourable reply and I look forward to hearing from you in due course.

Yours faithfully *(or Yours sincerely)*

Requesting Information from a College
Another example of a simple official letter is one to a college requesting information on a course which they run.

Dear Sir or Madam

For some time now I have been interested in doing a day-release course in joinery and carpentry.

I understand that you run such a course and I would be grateful to receive your latest prospectus and list of fees, together with any other relevant information. Enclosed is an s.a.e. for your convenience.

Yours faithfully

(An s.a.e. is a stamped addressed envelope to yourself.)

Confirming a Hotel Booking
You may have to write to a hotel or guest house confirming a booking for holiday accommodation. If you are writing to a large hotel, it is worth marking the letter (and envelope) "For The Attention Of: Reservations". When writing to a small guest house, it is probably sufficient to send your letter to the proprietor, as I have done in the following example:

Dear Mrs Burridge

Further to our telephone conversation today, I am pleased to confirm my booking for a double room with private bathroom for seven nights from 6th-11th September inclusive.

My wife and I will require bed, breakfast and evening meal facilities during our stay, and, as discussed, you will let us have a room with a sea view, if possible.

Enclosed is a cheque for the 10% deposit, and we look forward to seeing you all at Clifftops again in September.

With kindest regards and best wishes.

Yours sincerely

Courtesy Letter Thanking for Quotation

If you receive several quotations for the same job, it is always courteous to drop a line to those who were not successful in securing the job but who have, nevertheless, spent time on preparing their quotation. Such a letter could be as follows:

Dear Sirs

Thank you so much for sending the written quotation for the work which needs doing on my roof.

I have had several quotes for the repairs and I am afraid to say that I will not, on this occasion, be able to use your company to carry out the work. However, I just wanted to let you know the position and to thank you for your time and trouble.

Yours faithfully

You will notice that most of the letters in this section are quite short and to the point. It is always helpful to the reader (and it can save confusion) if your letters are concise.

7
Official Letters Requiring More Thought

As its name suggests, this chapter is concerned with letters which need more care, as very often the subject under discussion is of a sensitive nature. Or it could be that you are dissatisfied with a service of some kind and need to put your grievances in writing.

It may be worth mentioning that with this type of situation it is often better to try and deal with the matter verbally. The reasons are that it is generally a much more amicable way of handling a potential problem. If someone suddenly gets a letter (of complaint for example), the tone of the letter could actually make matters worse! There is also the time factor to take into account. If you deal with a matter verbally, you will know immediately where you stand, whereas if you send a letter there is always a period of delay while you wait for a reply.

However, there are times when something has to be put in writing, or a serious matter dealt with by correspondence. Very often, letters of this kind need to be longer than usual so that all the facts are laid out before the recipients to enable them to have a clear idea of the problem. It is therefore a good idea to keep notes of any meetings or telephone conversations so that all the relevant information is at your fingertips should you need to itemise certain points in a letter.

When writing such letters, it is worth bearing in mind:

(a) Do not write until you have calmly considered.
(b) Be courteous and concise, but you may need to be firm.

(c) Be patient and, if necessary, persistent.
(d) Don't worry *after* you have sent your letter.

I would *always* keep copies of this type of letter in order to refer back should the need arise. Keeping copies is especially important if you are threatening to take the matter further – to your solicitor, for example. (Also see Keeping Copies of Correspondence on page 76.)

The following are examples of letters covering a number of "difficult" situations.

Letters of Complaint

Complaint – Faulty Goods

Dear Sir

I was rather hoping that I would not have to write this letter, but I have been messed around so much by your staff that I feel the situation warrants a formal letter of complaint.

Last month I bought an electric kettle from your shop. Ever since getting it home it has been leaking, and despite my coming back about it several times your salesmen seem extremely reluctant to replace it.

Your Mr Greensmith initially offered to have it repaired for me, but I was not happy with this arrangement and I told him that I wanted a new appliance to replace the faulty one. You were out when I called and, to my astonishment, I was told by Mr Greensmith that he would have to consult you before a decision could be made. I believe I am entitled to a new appliance or a refund for faulty goods, under The Sale of Goods Act.

This is how the situation now stands, and I personally feel that this is a wholly unsatisfactory way of doing business; to say nothing of the damage to customer goodwill.

I will be calling into your shop on Friday and I will expect a new replacement kettle to be waiting for me. I trust you will advise your staff of these arrangements.

Yours faithfully

Complaint – To MP and to Local Council

On occasion, you may have to write to your MP or local council and I give below examples of letters to both of these. If you have to write to your MP, have a look at Chapter 2 for the correct way to address him or her.

Dear Sir

I have just come out of the Harlington Hospital and such is my concern with the conditions there that I felt I must inform you, as it could have far-reaching effects on other people in your constituency.

I was only in the hospital for three days while I had a minor operation on my foot, however, my three days were spent in what I can only describe as a dreadfully overcrowded, dirty ward (Craighouse Ward).

This may seem an exaggeration, but I can assure you that it is not. The ward was not only untidy and badly-kept – for example, dinner plates left uncleared for two hours on more than one occasion – but the sanitary facilities were disgusting. If I was presented with such facilities in a hotel, I would report it to the Health Inspector. Not only was there a general lack of cleanliness, but the food was horrendous. It was always lukewarm, badly cooked and totally unappetising – a bacterial paradise!

The doctors and nurses were very good indeed but were so obviously understaffed, and consequently overworked, that they were clearly unable to cope with the demands being put upon them.

I do hope you will investigate this matter urgently, as I feel the basic general hygiene of the hospital *must* be below the standard required. If this matter is not put right soon, I fear it could have serious consequences for elderly or very sick patients who could easily contract a serious infection as a result.

Yours faithfully

The following is a letter to the local council complaining about unkempt footpaths:

Dear Sirs

I have lived in Lower Meadington for over 20 years and was always proud of the way our town looked – until now. Over the last couple of years I have noticed a steady decline in standards on our highways and by-ways.

The footpaths in the town are now badly in need of repair. They are totally overgrown with weeds – not to mention all the accumulated rubbish. They are a major hazard to children and to the elderly who could easily have a serious accident. We now have an additional problem with wet leaves decaying in huge heaps along the paths, too. These could also cause an accident especially now that we have had so much rain in the last few days.

Could you please offer an explanation as to why our footpaths have been allowed to fall into such a state of disrepair and neglect? And, more importantly, what your department intends to do to rectify the situation.

I look forward to receiving your reply by return.

Yours faithfully

A copy of this letter should also be sent to your local councillor. Mention of this should be made in the form "Copy to..." below your signature.

Complaint – Neighbour's Noisy Dog

You may be in the unenviable position of having to write a letter of complaint to a neighbour. This one deals with the problem of a neighbour's noisy dog. I have started the letter "Dear Mr....", but you could start it "Dear Gerald", or whatever, if the person is someone you know very well.

Dear Mr Molton

On several occasions I have mentioned to you that your dog's constant barking during the night is causing us a great deal of disturbance.

I was hoping that we could settle this matter amicably, but it now seems to me that you are totally unable or unwilling to control your animal.

I am writing, therefore, to inform you that if a solution to this problem is not forthcoming within the next seven days, I very much regret that I will have no choice but to put the matter in the hands of my solicitor.

Yours sincerely

Letters of Campaign

If no results are forthcoming after many complaints your correspondence may become letters of campaign. You may want to protest about the proposal to build a new road through your quiet village or the one to build a new office block on the only 'green' site in your busy town. If it is an issue about which the relevant authority, your local councillor or MP are receiving much correspondence from many people of opposing views it is usually better to keep your letter short and to stick to one or two points, rather than to try to address the whole situation.

Dear Sirs

I hear you are considering the withdrawal of your nationwide milk and grocery delivery services.

As an OAP it would be quite impossible for me to walk one and a half miles uphill to the village shop if the doorstep pinta was discontinued. Am I not to be considered?

Yours faithfully

Dear Sirs

I do not believe Blandminster cattle market should be financed from public money. For instance, many people are opposed to the live export of calves for veal, and many are also vegetarian – are all these people prepared to contribute via their council tax for something they find morally offensive? It is easy for Councillor Jones to say that a few hundred enthusiasts would pay £20 extra on the town precept but to assume that a vocal minority at a meeting constitutes a majority of the population, as if in a referendum, is beyond belief!

It may be his political party's interpretation but it is not democratic.

Yours faithfully

Letter Supporting an Insurance Claim
A fairly common letter is one to an insurance company supporting a claim. In this example, the writer is querying why his insurers have declined to pay the full amount for a coat which has been completely destroyed by fire.

Dear Sirs

In reply to your letter offering £75 compensation against the coat which was recently burned, and which had been bought two months ago for £225, I must ask you to reconsider the matter.

In twenty-one years I have never made a claim and have paid you in premiums many hundreds of pounds. Do you consider your offer of £75 against a coat worth £225 is fair?

I did not claim the larger sum with any intention of entering into negotiation for its reduction, because the coat had only been worn twice and was obviously still worth its original value, or within a few pounds of it.

Unless you send the £225 within the next ten days, my policy will be transferred to another insurer, and I will be instructing my solicitor to take legal action to recover the £225 from your company.

I await your reply and trust that it will contain an explanation that some mistake has been made by your office.

Yours faithfully

It is worth mentioning that unless you really intend going to your solicitor, do not make the threat. In other words, never indicate that you will do something unless you are prepared to do it.

Child Being Bullied at School

Another difficult situation in which you may need to write a letter could be where your child is being bullied at school. The example I have given is where the bullying is being done by a teacher, so a letter is being written "In Strictest Confidence" (envelope the same) to the head. You could adapt this letter if your child was being bullied by another pupil.

Dear Mr Jenkinson

Over the last few weeks I have become increasingly concerned about Jeremy. His school work has deteriorated and he has been sullen and withdrawn at home. Despite my trying to talk to him about this on numerous occasions, he would not discuss it with me.

However, things came to a head last night, and to my horror I discovered the reason for Jeremy's change in character is that one of your teachers is bullying and belittling him – both publicly and in private. The teacher in question is John Leonard – Jeremy's new maths teacher. When I asked Jeremy why he was being victimised in this way, he felt it was because he was not very good at maths and was falling behind most of his classmates in the subject. (However, it would appear that there are two others who are also being penalised in this way.)

As I am sure you will appreciate, these are very serious allegations, however I have no reason to disbelieve my son. I know that you will want to investigate this matter thoroughly and may need to interview both Jeremy and myself, and we will be pleased to discuss the matter further with you at any time.

However, I would like to receive your assurance, by

return, that this matter will be looked into immediately. Also, I must insist that Jeremy is removed at once from this teacher's classes.

I would like to add that I will not tolerate a situation such as this, and if my son continues to be victimised in this way I will not only remove him from your school, but I will feel duty-bound to inform the school governors and the local education authority of my reasons for doing so.

I look forward to receiving your reply.

Yours sincerely

Defaulting on Mortgage Repayments

Finally I deal with a letter which we all hope we will never have to write; about defaulting on mortgage repayments. It is worth bearing in mind that if you find yourself in such a situation, a letter is better written sooner rather than later, as it is most unwise to let matters like this drift on and on. However, in my example letter, I am assuming that the writer has been hoping things would get better, which is why he has put off writing his letter.

Dear Mr Crawford

I sincerely regret having to write this letter, and have been delaying it in the hope that things would improve. However, as the outlook is still very bleak, I felt it best to get in touch and put you in the picture.

The problem, quite simply, is that my wife and I are finding it impossible, at present, to keep up with the current level of mortgage repayments on our home.

Two months ago, I was made redundant (I was given one week's notice) from my job which I had held for over fifteen years. As you can appreciate, it has not been easy trying to find alternative employment in the same trade, and now, in desperation, I have taken a job working at the local hypermarket. The problem is that my wages are now a third less than they used to be, and because we are already behind with our repayments I can see no way that we can "catch up" again, let alone pay the money we are now in arrears. My wife can only work part-time, and the money she earns is spent on feeding the family.

I am very sorry about this, and wondered if it would be possible for us to meet and discuss the situation. Perhaps we could work something out whereby my wife and I could pay you a reduced amount, but over a longer period, or something of that sort.

Once again, my sincere apologies for all of this, but I hope we can meet and get it sorted out very soon.

Yours sincerely

8
Applying for a Job

A letter applying for a job is probably one of the most important you will ever have to write; and its style, presentation and content could have a strong bearing on the decisions of any potential employer.

When applying for a job, the state of your handwriting is often considered to be a reflection of your personality. A neatly-written, well set out letter could make the difference between your getting an interview or not. In some jobs, neat handwriting is of vital importance, for instance in occupations where legible and tidily-written numbers are imperative.

If you have several qualifications and a good deal of work experience, you may wish to compose your own Curriculum Vitae (CV). This is a brief resumé of the schools/colleges you have attended with qualifications gained, together with personal information and brief details of your career to date. It would be quite correct to send a typed CV, but it is worth noting that most employers would prefer to see it accompanied by a hand-written covering letter.

There are, however, still a few occasions when a letter, containing all the relevant information, could be used in preference to a CV.

When writing a letter of this kind, the secret is to be brief and to the point. Try only to include information which is relevant to the job for which you are applying. Don't write page after page of waffle, with details which will be of no interest to the reader, or your letter is likely just to be cast aside. An over long letter giving vast details of your past and present life will probably count against you.

One of the most common ways in which we hear about job vacancies is through newspaper advertisements, and these would normally require a letter of application. Before replying, read the advertisement with great care and make sure that all the information requested is supplied in your answer.

Job application letters can be difficult as it is not always known to whom one is writing because some advertisements appear under the name of a management consultancy, an employment agency or a box or telephone number.

Not all applications are in reply to advertisements. There is, of course, the method of writing to a particular firm in the line of business which the applicant is anxious to enter. When he knows the person to whom he is writing he can formulate some idea of the *type* of letter likely to appeal; and as individuals differ so much, there is little to be gained by elaboration here.

I must now stress several points in connection with such letters:

Firstly, keep your application as short as is consistent with the information required.

Secondly, study the wording of the advertisement carefully because from it you may be able to judge much about the advertiser. The old-fashioned firm of wine merchants, seeking a representative for the Midlands, will probably be best approached by an impersonal letter, carefully phrased, giving all details asked for and full particulars of your career. On the other hand, the firm looking for a "live-wire" salesman possessing initiative, drive and a forceful personality, could receive an application worded in a lighter and more aggressive vein, though I must add that it is safer to err on the side of dignity than the reverse.

Thirdly, the applicant must read the requirements for the post closely and in his reply must state clearly which he is able to fulfil. He must also ensure that he has answered the advertisement *fully;* for instance, if he is asked to state the salary required he should not evade the question.

Perhaps the most important factor in an application is the *tone* of the letter, and in general the applicant is well advised to show keenness for the post. One reason for keeping your application short is that if you give too many particulars, you may thereby jeopardise your chances of an interview.

Here are some sample advertisements followed by appropriate replies, to give you an idea of what is required.

(a) Advertisement

Senior PA required for young art director of international ad. agency. Needs someone to organise him totally and look after the office when he's away. First class shorthand and typing speeds, WP and organisational skills essential. Ad. agency experience preferred. Age 25+. Excellent salary for right person. Contact Jason Davies, Personnel Manager, Actionads Ltd., 3 Wray's Walk, Croydon, Surrey CR9 0LS.

Reply

Dear Mr Davies

Further to your advertisement in yesterday's Croydon Courier for a senior PA, I would very much like to be considered for this vacancy.

I am 28 years old, and have worked as a senior level P.A. for the past eight years; most recently for John Charlton, art director of Artlines Advertising Agency in London. Although I have been very happy at Artlines for the past four years, I am keen to find work which is nearer to my new home in Purley.

For the last eleven years I have worked exclusively in advertising, so feel that the experience I have gained will be of great value in your company.

In my present job I regularly cover for Mr Charlton in his absence, when I am responsible for the day-to-day running of the office, the answering of correspondence, and the supervision of two junior members of our support team.

After leaving Croydon High School with eight "O" levels, I studied for two years at The Lawns Secretarial College in Selhurst, where I gained certificates for 100 w.p.m. shorthand, and advanced level typing. My present shorthand and typing speeds are 110 w.p.m. and 70 w.p.m. respectively, and I have a good working knowledge of the Wordstar, Multimate and Word Perfect word processing systems.

I do hope to hear from you soon.

Yours sincerely

(b) Advertisement

Lady or gentleman required for school crossing patrol at St. Mark's Junior School, New Town. Would suit active senior citizen. Hours: 8.00–9.15 a.m. and 3.00–4.15 p.m., Monday – Friday. Uniform provided. Excellent rates of pay. Please contact The Works Manager, New Town District Council, The Town Hall, 23 High Street, New Town, Wiltshire, SN8 9AG.

Reply

Dear Sir

I am writing with regard to your vacancy for a school crossing patrol person at St. Mark's Junior School, as advertised in this week's New Town Messenger.

Since retiring last December I have been looking for a suitable part-time job and feel that your vacancy is ideal, as St. Mark's is just round the corner from where I live. I do not have any other regular commitments on my time, so I could easily be available during the hours which you state.

I know many of the parents whose children attend St. Mark's, as my two grandchildren are pupils there.

Before I retired, I was a traffic warden for fifteen years, so I am well aware of road safety and traffic regulations which I think would be useful in this post.

My hobbies are walking, gardening and DIY and I consider myself to be very fit and active for my age.

I do hope that I will be successful, and that I may hear from you in the near future.

Yours faithfully

(c) Advertisement

Gardener required for about two days a week for a one-acre garden in Colchester. Small orchard, vegetable plot, greenhouse and flower beds to tend. All equipment provided. Hours to suit. Excellent rates of pay, plus meals and share of produce. Please reply to Box 35, Colchester Courier Newspaper Group, 254 Green Street, Colchester, Essex, CO1 1YY.

Reply

Dear Sir or Madam

I was most interested to read your advertisement for a gardener, and feel I could be just the person for your vacancy.

Ten months ago, I moved to Colchester from Norwich where I had been employed for four years as a landscape gardener with Logan Landscapes. I also have a Certificate in Horticultural Studies.

Since moving to Colchester, I have been a self-employed jobbing gardener, but I now have two days a week to spare since one of the people I worked for has died.

Should you require a reference, please feel free to get in touch with Mr David Logan at Logan Landscapes, 10 Quarry Street, Norwich, Norfolk, NR5 9BU, who will be happy to help you.

I look forward to hearing from you soon.

Yours faithfully

(d) Advertisement

Junior required to work in friendly office/warehouse. Work will include filing, photocopying, packing orders and general office duties. Age 16–19. Good general education required, but no qualifications or experience necessary as full training will be given. Good starting salary with reviews every six months.

Please apply to Mr Peter Endell, The Redbridge Clothing Company, Redbridge Road, Liverpool, L45 8UX.

Reply

Dear Mr Endell

With reference to your advertisement in today's Liverpool Echo, I would very much like to be considered for the vacancy of office junior in your company.

I am 16 years old and will be leaving Middleham School at the end of next week, as I will then have finished my GCSE examinations.

For the past year I have worked as a Saturday sales assistant at Charisma Fashions in Liverpool who stock many of your lines, so I am quite familiar with your range of garments. Mrs Grant, the manageress at Charisma, has offered to give me a reference if you require one.

It has always been my wish to have a career in the clothing industry, and I would be grateful for the opportunity to talk to you about the vacancy you have available.

I do hope that I may be considered for the job, and that you may invite me for interview in the near future.

Yours sincerely

Advertisement
Old-established London publishing firm, with long list of successful works of fiction, requires sales representative to cover Scotland, Northern Ireland and the North of England. Must live in Glasgow. Reply stating experience, age and salary required. Box No. 31158.

Reply

Box No. 31158

Please treat in strict confidence

Dear Sirs

In answer to your advertisement in today's issue of the Glasgow Herald, I give below the particulars requested.

1. I am at present employed with Plowden & Monck

Limited, of London, having been with them for three years as their representative covering the territories mentioned in your advertisement. My only reason for wishing to make a change is that I may improve my position. Prior to my present work, I learned the business with Atkinson & Finlay Limited and was with them for seven years, during the last three of which I was Sales Representative in the Midlands.

2. Age: 36.

3. I am asking a salary of £xxxxx per annum, but if it is your wish to pay on a salary plus commission basis, I should be pleased to discuss the matter with you.

4. May I stress that I am particularly interested in the fiction market and have considerable experience of it. I know the buyers well in the areas I have covered.

I hope that I may be granted an interview.

Yours faithfully

Applying for an Unadvertised Job

There is no doubt, of course, that many positions are filled which are never advertised. Sometimes one hears of jobs which are open or likely to be open, and a visit to the employer may prove successful. In other cases, a letter may have to be written, and it should be kept short and give brief but full particulars. The letter could be composed in a variety of ways, and here is an example.

Dear Sirs

I am writing to enquire whether your company has any vacancies in your invoicing department, since I am keen to obtain work as an invoice clerk. Below are particulars of my previous experience:

The details can then be listed and that is all there is to it. Conclude with:

I do hope to hear from you and I enclose a stamped addressed envelope for your reply.

Yours faithfully

Writing to a firm that conducts business in which you are particularly interested sometimes brings satisfactory results. It is, of course, a "hit or miss" method, but there is always the chance that your application may coincide with a decision to increase staff, or there may be a vacancy to fill.

Dear Sir or Madam

I write to enquire if you have an opening for a sales representative.

I was educated at the King's School, Chester, leaving at 17, and have since been employed by Edward J Kellett & Company Limited, of Manchester, until a week ago, when the firm closed down. I worked in their Order and Accounts Department, and am therefore accustomed to trade terms, calculations and market trends. I have also a fairly extensive knowledge of the different kinds of timber.

I am most anxious to become a sales representative because I have a keen interest in timber and its uses, am fond of travelling and able to make contacts easily.

I enclose a copy of my curriculum vitae which gives further information.

If you have a suitable vacancy on your staff, I should be grateful if you would grant me an interview.

Yours faithfully

Applying for a Job in Another District

There is also the case where someone may need to move to a new district and have to find employment in a particular trade. The best way is probably to write to the companies in the trade you wish to enter (if there are not too many of them) in the new locality, and an example of such a letter is given here:

Dear Sirs

I will soon be moving into your area from Dorset and am writing to enquire whether you have any vacancies for retail hi-fi sales staff within your company. I have a wide experience in this business, and I am therefore hoping to continue my employment in this field. Full particulars of my previous experience are given below: (*list of particulars*)

You could conclude:

I would be most grateful to hear if there is any opening in your firm for which I might be suitable. Failing that, I would be obliged if you could advise me of any other firms to whom you think it might be worth while my writing. I enclose a stamped addressed envelope and thank you in anticipation.

Yours faithfully

9

Introductions, References and Resignations

Introductions

Although these are rarely used nowadays, except possibly for journeys abroad (when they may be written on behalf of a traveller who is covering fresh territory or to establish identity), it is still useful to know a bit about them. Their purpose is to introduce one person or body of persons to another; they should be brief, courteous and to the point.

When writing an introductory letter, always take great care to ensure that the wording is accurate so that no false assumptions can be arrived at by the recipient. Considerable importance might be attached to the fact that you had gone to the trouble of giving an introduction, and it might be thought that because of this you knew the party to be absolutely reliable, which might not always be the case.

Below is an example of a letter of introduction for someone that the writer knows very well who has emigrated.

Dear Peter and Jenny,

I do hope you and the boys are all well and that life "Down-Under" is keeping you all busy.

My reason for writing is that some of my close friends have just moved out to Australia and, coincidentally, are living in Melbourne. Their names are Roger and Jackie

Brampton. I have known them for over ten years and they were, in fact, my next door neighbours for six years. They have three children – Emma (8), Billy (5) and Sam (2). Roger is a civil engineer and has got a job in Melbourne working for S.C.G., which I believe is the biggest engineering firm there. The company have found them a house, and their address is: Box 63, Wongalong Road, Melbourne.

As they have no relatives or friends in Australia, I said I would write and ask if you would get in touch with them. Maybe you could give them a few hints about the locality and that sort of thing? It would really help them get started. I know you'll love them – they're a smashing family!

I would be so grateful if you'd do this for me, and look forward to hearing how you all get along.

Will write a long letter soon.

With love and best wishes...

Another type of introductory letter might be one written for someone seeking employment, but apart from this, most other forms of introduction would probably be done over the telephone; for example, you might introduce a friend to a reputable firm of builders.

For the attention of Mr William Paul
Firm Foundations Limited
7–11 Westminster Steps
London
SW9 7UZ

Dear Mr Paul

Mr David Brett, who has been with us for two-and-a-half years as an apprentice draughtsman, is most anxious to enter the building trade, and it occurs to me that you may be able to help him, either by considering his capabilities if you happen to have a suitable vacancy in your own firm, or by advising him as to the best method of obtaining the kind of work for which he is looking.

Needless to say, I shall be very pleased if you can do anything for Mr Brett; during his service with us he has been perfectly satisfactory.

Yours sincerely
SMITH & JONES LIMITED

John Smith

Tempest Agricultural Sundries Company
266 Kenyatta Concourse
Nairobi
Kenya

Dear Sirs

I am writing to introduce Mr John Jackson, our agricultural representative, in the hope that you may be able to offer him some assistance.

Mr Jackson is making a study of crop yields in certain areas of Kenya and I shall be extremely grateful if you are able to give him any information which will help him carry out his work.

Yours faithfully
HUGHES & HUGHES LIMITED

Simon K Medway

Do not give introductions too freely as there may be repercussions, and be particularly careful if you recommend somebody as being trustworthy; human nature being what it is, there is a danger in assumptions. My remarks under this heading will be reinforced when I deal with the writing of references.

References

It would be impossible to overstress the importance of the wording of a reference letter, because a great deal can depend upon it.

Basically, there are two types of reference. There is the open reference (more correctly known as a testimonial) which someone leaving takes with them, and I feel that this is not really worth much unless the recipient knows something about the writer of the reference. My reason for this is simply that it is always assumed that a lot of praise is put into the letter, possibly more out of kindness than because it is deserved.

The other, more valuable, reference is the one which is obtained by the prospective employer writing direct to the former employer asking any particular questions he might wish answered. There is, however, a potential danger here that an employer could write a good reference for an employee because he wants to be rid of him (or her)! Generally speaking, though, employers are fair-minded and give an honest reference – to protect their professional integrity if nothing else!

Having said that, I personally never attach too much value to any reference, the reason being that although a person may have done badly in a previous job, it does not follow that he will do badly in the next one. Working conditions may vary and such is the nature of personal relationships that employees who cannot work satisfactorily for one person, very often can for another. Also, it often follows that if an employee has not done very well in a previous job, he has learnt a lesson and will do much better in the new one.

Take Care What You Write

The composition of a testimonial calls for knowledge and care. This fixed rule should be observed: never write a testimonial unless the person for whom it is written has been known to you for a considerable time, and you possess a good deal of information about him. One is apt to write testimonials out of kindness, but remember that what you say may carry considerable weight and may influence some extremely important decision. The result may be far from kindness to someone!

Some years ago, a friend of mine, a leading figure in his industry, was asked by a life-long friend to write a reference for the latter's son. Apart from an occasional meeting, this young man was unknown to him, but in view of the long friendship between the boy's father and himself, he willingly agreed to write a letter of introduction somewhat on the following lines:

Fansham House
Chagford
Devon, TQ4 8LK

5 August XXXX

This letter is to introduce Mr Roy X; I hope you will be able to do something to help him obtain satisfactory work. He is a hard-working, honest and energetic young man.

The statement on his capabilities and character was simply repeated from what his father had said. On the strength of this introduction, the young man obtained an important post in a large concern and everything appeared to be satisfactory. About two years later, however, my friend received a letter from one of the directors of the company informing him that Mr X had embezzled a large sum of money and had subsequently disappeared, taking with him a lot of property belonging to the firm. I quote this unfortunate incident as an illustration of the pitfalls into which one may be lured. As the whole subject is of such importance, I propose to outline the procedure which it would normally be reasonably safe to follow.

The Writing of References

Business people today usually want a concise summary of the individual concerned. I would think that the old-fashioned type of reference, several pages long, which was concerned with things like length of service, qualities of character and so on, is rarely used nowadays. Many larger companies often just send out a standard questionnaire for the former employer to fill in.

If you are ever asked to write a reference you should be guided by the following points:

(a) absolute accuracy
(b) brevity.

Another very important point it is worth noting is that *all* reference letters should be marked "Private and Confidential", as should the envelopes in which you send them.

Below are some different examples of the sort of wording you could use if writing references for good employees.

(a) Catrina Kelly is leaving us as our secretary as she is moving away from this area. She is a conscientious and dedicated member of our team and her work has always been excellent.

(b) Darren Gale is leaving us because his career has advanced as far as possible within our company. He has been in charge of our buying department for three years and has been a very able and competent manager. We have no vacancy higher up so cannot give him the promotion he deserves. We are very sorry to lose him, but wish him every success in the future.

(c) Joanna Black has been our senior sales manager for

five years and is leaving us because our wholesale department has been sold. We are very pleased to be able to say that Joanna has injected enormous energy and flair into all her projects, and we have no hesitation in recommending her for your vacancy.

This type of reference is comparatively easy, but we now come to the problem of giving a reference to a person who has been less satisfactory as an employee. This is a very difficult matter because naturally an employer does not like to condemn someone who may have been unsatisfactory in the past. The best line to take with somebody who has not been *too bad* is to write something like:

Simon Green is leaving us because he needs a higher salary than we feel able to pay him. He has been with us for two years and we have always found him trustworthy and wish him success in the future.

There is also the much more difficult instance of the employee who has been dishonest and thoroughly unsatisfactory. If such an employee asks you for a reference he can take away with him when he leaves, the best thing to do is to refuse to give one, but to say that you are willing to supply one to a prospective employer.

If you do this it is extremely unlikely that the person concerned will ever give your name to a future employer because he would not expect a good reference, and if he is dishonest he will probably make up some story or provide a bogus reference. (It might interest you to know that the employees who have swindled me, and there have been a few, were the ones who provided the most wonderful references as to their integrity, etc.)

In giving an adverse reference regarding an employee, you would be entitled to state the facts fully but accurately, provided the letter is addressed personally to the enquirer. It is most important in this instance that the letter (and envelope) be marked “Private and

Confidential". However, you must be extremely cautious when writing references of this nature. Even in a confidential letter, if anything was said which was out of malice or spite, however tempted you might be, the legal position might prove very dangerous. (See The Risks of Letter Writing, page 56.)

If you find yourself in a position where you have to give an adverse reference, let me offer you a word of advice. It is always much better to give a bad reference by word of mouth than in writing, and the line to take is to tell the truth about the person, but without malice, as even verbally, the legal position is always uncertain.

Open References/Testimonials

When you are asked to give an open reference, it is wiser to offer to supply one against an enquiry from an employer. There are, of course, instances where some form of recommendation is required for the purpose of showing to potential employers, and if the man or woman has been known to you over a number of years it would probably be safe to agree. You can do this without committing yourself to any statement which may have serious repercussions later.

Many references begin by stating the employee's length of service, the different kinds of work carried out, and so forth, but they are often too protracted and thereby lose much of their effect. The old custom of heading the statement: "To Whom It May Concern" need not be followed. All that is called for is a signed statement underneath a printed letter heading somewhat as follows:

THE EUREKA TANDEM COMPANY LIMITED
Hanworth Works, Station Road
Coventry
West Midlands, CV7 8QQ

3 June XXXX

Mr Frank Wells has been employed by us as a Sales Manager for five years and we have found him to be honest. He is a man of great energy and considerable initiative. We believe that anything he undertakes will be carried out to the best of his ability.

(Signed)

TOMKINSON, DANIEL & TOMKINSON
3 Queen Square
Aberdeen, AB5 9XL

3 June XXXX

Miss Patricia Burke has been employed by us for the past two years as a shorthand-typist and we have found her to be entirely trustworthy. Her work has always been satisfactory.

(Signed)

As stated earlier, in the event of an employer being asked for a testimonial by an untrustworthy or unsatisfactory employee, the safest reply is to explain that you have a general rule never to supply open references but will be pleased to answer any questions from future employers. On the other hand, it is always possible to give an innocuous letter on the following lines:

TOMKINSON, DANIEL & TOMKINSON
3 Queen Square
Aberdeen, AB5 9XL

3 June XXXX

Mr Thomas Blagdon has been with this firm as a clerk for

eighteen months and is leaving because he wishes to go abroad.

If an employee has been untrustworthy, it would be dangerous to give as brief a reference as the above, as it implies some degree of confidence where none, in fact, existed. When in doubt, it is generally wise to refuse to give your employee any sort of reference; there is no legal obligation to do so.

When handing an employee a satisfactory reference you are on reasonably safe ground, but if you make a statement somewhat on the following lines – "Miss A B Smith has been with us for five years and, *apart from her poor health,* has been quite satisfactory." – you might be courting serious trouble. Your statement might be held in law to be malicious libel. On the other hand, if you are answering an enquiry about it from a potential employer you are privileged and allowed comparatively wide scope, provided your reply *and the envelope* are marked "Private and Confidential". However, "the law is an ass", so you will be wise to give any adverse comments over the telephone or, more safely, by a personal discussion. Even telephone calls can be "tapped", and if you suspect that there are other listeners, be on your guard. Always remember that your comments, whether verbal or written, must be made in good faith. For example:

28 July XXXX

PRIVATE AND CONFIDENTIAL
Mr Alfred J Shannon
Personnel Director
Shannon & Brewster Limited
Change Court
River Street
Aberdeen
AB9 5RT

Dear Mr Shannon

In reply to your enquiry of 26 July XXXX, concerning Miss May Hanworth, who has been employed by us for three months, we released her because we found her work to be generally unsatisfactory. She was inclined to be late for work on a number of occasions and caused a certain amount of trouble among the rest of our staff.

Yours sincerely

Andrew Smith

Admittedly, such a reference is extremely damning and would almost certainly jeopardise the girl's chances of obtaining a good post elsewhere, but your remarks – being, from your point of view, a true statement – could safely be committed to paper so long as they are marked "Private and Confidential" and are addressed to a senior official of the firm. Human nature being what it is, however, you would be wise to tone down your remarks as follows:

28 July XXXX

PRIVATE AND CONFIDENTIAL
Mr Alfred J Shannon
Personnel Director
Shannon & Brewster Limited
Change Court
River Street
Aberdeen
AB9 5RT

Dear Mr Shannon

In reply to your enquiry of 26 July XXXX, concerning

Miss May Hanworth, who has been employed by us for three months as a shorthand-typist, we are sorry to have to say that we did not find her suitable. Quite possibly she will do better with another employer.

Yours sincerely

Andrew Smith

Fortunately, most people know why they have been given notice, and they will probably try to avoid giving their last employers as a reference.

The Value of References

The only occasion where a reference is really of value is when the writer is known personally to the person for whom it is produced. An open reference under an unknown letter heading and over an equally unknown signature cannot be expected to carry much weight. Most people quite naturally like to give a good reference whenever they can, so that such open testimonials have of necessity lost much value.

It is never wise to send an *original* testimonial with an application; it might become lost or for some other reason you might never get it back. Always send a copy, marked accordingly. The original can be produced at a subsequent interview, but do not let it leave your possession.

Appointments

As a rule, these are simple and straightforward letters confirming verbal arrangements made at an interview.

In a book such as this I cannot deal fully with contracts of employment; sufficient to remark that such contracts are tricky for both sides. I remember a friend, and a solicitor at that, making a partnership contract with a sick old man of 80. My 47-year-old friend joined the old boy on a contract to work for nothing during the aged one's business life, thereafter he was to get the entire business for nothing. Result? My friend died at 60 while the old rascal was still in business at 93 and did not give my friend's widow a penny for 13 years of hard work!

The Contracts of Employment Acts

In July 1964 the original Act relating to Contracts of Employment came into effect. Since that time it has been amended several times and new legislation introduced.

The aims of these Acts are to protect employees from unscrupulous practices and to make sure that all employers give employees full details, in writing, of their terms and conditions of employment. Written advice of pay increases/decreases must also be given to the employees as the changes occur. See page 248 for more details about Contracts of Employment.

Official notes are available from the Department of Employment for the guidance of employers.

I now give an example of a letter offering employment.

SMITH & WILSON LIMITED
Hurstmoncieux Buildings, Vale Avenue
Blackpool, FY1 1DL

21 May XXXX

Mr D R J Black
123 Bedford Avenue
Blackpool
FY1 7DG

Dear Mr Black

We are writing to confirm our verbal arrangement that you should start work with us on June XXXX, at 9am, at a commencing salary of £xxx per week, subject to the standard conditions of employment laid down by Acts of

Parliament, brief details of which you will find in the enclosed copy.

Please be kind enough to confirm this appointment.

Yours sincerely

J R Smith

This example is a simple confirmation of appointment; but a special statement must be drawn up, embodying specific terms of service – this is dealt with on page 249, under 'Contracts'.

Resignations
As a rule, the acceptance of a resignation, on an official basis, is a simple matter and merely states the facts. I give first a specimen letter tendering a resignation and follow it with the official acceptance.

Dear Mr Jones

On the recommendation of my medical adviser, I am regretfully obliged to tender my resignation from the staff of the Britannia Engine Company with effect from 31 July XXXX, and hereby give one month's notice in accordance with the terms of my contract.

Yours sincerely

Letters on similar lines may involve directors' or partners' resignations.

Dear Mr Smith

It is with regret that we accept your resignation from our staff, to take effect from 31 July XXXX. We are very sorry it has been necessary to take this step and hope that your health may soon improve.

Yours sincerely
THE BRITANNIA ENGINE COMPANY LIMITED

A Jones
Personnel Officer

There follows another example of a resignation letter which you may write to an employer when you wish to leave your job. This type of letter is quite straightforward to write and should be as concise as possible.

Dear Mr Harrison

It is with much regret that I have to write and inform you of my wish to resign from my current position. I have always enjoyed my work with your company, but feel that the time has come when I would like to have a job in a new field. I have been offered a vacancy locally, so would like to leave in one month's time, as required by my contract.

Yours sincerely

The most important thing to say about resignations is that they are often accepted, therefore do not resign from something in a fit of temper if you do not really want to.

Never write a letter of resignation (or indeed for any

other purpose) *in the heat of the moment* and live to regret it. Make a draft, by all means, then leave it for a day or so. You may later change your mind, or circumstances may change it for you.

If you have to resign from the committee of a club or society, this is dealt with in the next chapter.

Letters on Retirement

When a director of a company, or a representative perhaps, retires it is often difficult to think of something nice to say which is just a little bit out of the ordinary, but which will be cherished by the recipient. What can be said of course depends very much on the circumstances, but a little bit of flattery goes down well and flattery can be true as well as false. Here is a sample:

Dear John

I find it very hard to believe you are retiring and I am sure you will have many interests which will fully occupy the leisure which you so much deserve.

Your company is losing a great asset. I remember the day when you arrived at our office to find us struggling with a burst pipe and how you helped us to bail out the water. Then there was the day when I took ill and at inconvenience to yourself you so kindly drove me 15 miles home.

But I will most remember you for all the useful and free advice you have offered us; it is not too much to say that we would not be here today if we hadn't accepted it.

Once again, wishing you every possible happiness in your retirement and hoping that if you ever pass our road you will come in for a chat.

Yours very sincerely
JONES & SMITH LIMITED

Richard Jones
Director

Letters of Congratulation

Such letters are often more difficult than they appear. You may have a *flair* for this type of letter and will in that case probably be in demand! Most people will find a simple straightforward letter the easiest way of coping with the situation.

The custom of sending congratulatory letters has diminished in the last few years, although when someone wins public acclamation in a particular field, obtains academic distinction, becomes engaged or gets married, a message of goodwill and congratulation may be called for.

Engagements, marriages, births and business promotions generally present an occasion for a short letter, which may be on the following lines:

Dear Mr Jackson

I am delighted to hear of your new appointment to the Board. The many years you have worked with the Company have been rewarded, and my partner and I send you our very best wishes for the future.

Yours sincerely
SIMPKIN & HUDSON LIMITED

J G Simpkin
Director

Dear Mr Blagdon

I saw the announcement of the birth of your daughter in "The Daily Telegraph" this morning, and I am writing to send my congratulations and best wishes to you and your wife.

I do hope your wife is progressing favourably and will soon be at home again.

Yours sincerely

Stephen Browne

Dear Sir Robert

We were so pleased to see from the Honours List that your outstanding work as a Civil Engineer has been suitably rewarded, and send you our congratulations.

Yours sincerely

Martin Yates

10

Clubs, Societies and Letters to "The Editor"

Local Clubs and Societies

Many of us are members of clubs and societies in our local areas – squash or tennis clubs, conservation groups, amateur dramatic societies, family history societies, over-60s clubs – the choice is many and varied.

Applying for Membership

The procedure for joining these various activities will vary from group to group, but I will start by giving a simple letter which you could use when applying for membership of, say, a local squash club. This letter would be sent to the Membership Secretary.

Dear Sir or Madam

I have just moved to this area and am writing to enquire whether I may become a member of the Brayside Squash Club.

My standard of play is generally thought to be better than average, as I am currently top of the second division in the Club league at the Calverley Squash Club in north London, where I have been a member for the last three years.

Please could you let me know if there is a waiting list, as I am most anxious to join your club right away. I would be grateful if you could let me know your annual fee charges and any other information which would be useful.

I look forward to hearing from you in the near future. Please find enclosed a stamped, self-addressed envelope for your reply.

Yours faithfully

You will note from the above that the writer sends an s.a.e. with his letter. I firmly believe that this can make a big difference. Not only will it speed up the postal side of your reply, but people often feel 'obliged' to reply to you! It could also mean that your letter may be put to the top of the pile for reply. There are, in fact, many reasons why sending an s.a.e. is a good idea, not least that it is a courteous gesture which is usually much appreciated by the recipient.

Joining a Committee

There may come a time when you are asked to join the committee of a local group, or you may volunteer and be elected at its Annual General Meeting. Depending on your role, you may have to correspond with various people on behalf of the group.

Booking a Guest Speaker

As a member of a committee, you may be responsible for booking guest speakers, who should always get a confirmatory letter. An example of such a letter follows.

Dear Mr Jarvis

Further to our telephone conversation, I am delighted that you have kindly agreed to give an illustrated talk to our Group on the subject of "Wildlife In Surrey", on the 6th of next month.

The meeting will be held at St. Peter's Hall, Lower Road, Redhill, starting at 8.00 p.m., so if you could arrive a few minutes before this it will give you time to get settled in.

We would be grateful if your talk could last approximately 30-45 minutes. After this, there will be a break for refreshments, followed by a questions session which usually lasts for about 30 minutes. You mentioned that you will not require a slide projector as you will be bringing all your own equipment.

As discussed, you do not require a fee for your talk, but would only need a small payment towards your travel expenses.

Finally, I enclose a sketch map showing how to get to the hall, and I very much look forward to seeing you next month. Please do not hesitate to get in touch if you need to discuss this further.

With very best wishes and thanks.

Yours sincerely

Mrs Jane T McFarlane
Programme Organiser
North Downs Conservation Group

At the top of the letter you need to put your own address (unless the group has an 'official' address), and the address of the recipient; don't forget the date! It would also be helpful to them if you included your telephone number. If you have a phone number for the person to whom you are writing, it is always a good idea to jot this down on your copy of the letter. Also, note from the above how you should close a letter of this kind, putting your name, 'job' title and name of your group along with your signature. If your letter needs a reply, include an s.a.e.

You will see that my example contains *all* the information that may be needed in the future. The reason for this is that many such speakers (especially the best ones!) are booked up for months, and sometimes years, in advance. It is therefore vitally important that (a) such a confirmatory letter is sent, and (b) every scrap of information is included. With the passage of time, it is easy to forget the details of verbal arrangements. If you book a speaker a long way in advance, it is always wise to check nearer the time that they are still able to give the talk – either by sending a short follow-up letter, or by giving them a quick call.

Thanking a Guest Speaker
It is customary, and good manners, to write a short note of thanks to any guest speaker who may visit your group. This letter should always be sent the day after the talk. Remember to insert your name, position on the committee and name of the group at the bottom of the letter, as the speaker (especially if he/she is popular) may visit several groups each week. The following is an example of the type of letter which is required.

Dear Mrs Applegarth

On behalf of the ladies of the Lowfield W.I., I would just like to say how very much we enjoyed your talk yesterday evening. Not only was it highly amusing, but your floral creations were delightful.

Thank you so much for coming to speak to us, and I do hope you may be able to pay us a return visit in the future to talk to us about one of your other horticultural specialities.

With best wishes and thanks once again.

Yours sincerely

You would then put your name, position, and the name of the group.

Leaving the Committee
There is bound to come a time when you will have to leave the committee. There may be various reasons – perhaps you cannot now spare the time, or you feel it's time to let someone else have a go, or maybe you are moving away from the area. I have used this last reason in the following example of a letter which could be used when you have to resign from a committee.

Dear Stuart

As you know, I am leaving the district in two months' time, so it is with great regret that I will have to resign as Secretary of the Downs Cricket Club.

I would like to take this opportunity to say how much I have enjoyed being a member of the committee; I shall miss all the very good friends I have made.

May I send you all my very best wishes for the future; I shall be keeping in touch so will continue to follow the Club's progress with interest!

Yours

This letter would be sent to the Chairman of the Committee.

There are obviously many other letters which you could write on behalf of a local group or society, but I hope the ones above demonstrate how to deal with the sort of detailed and unusual things you are likely to come across.

Letters to "The Editor"

As the name suggests, these are letters covering a wide range of subjects which are written to the editors of national and regional newspapers, or magazines, by members of the public.

Generally speaking, it is very difficult to get a letter printed in a national daily newspaper and particularly in one of the "serious", "heavyweight" newspapers such as *The Times* or *The Daily Telegraph*. But people do, and if you are aspiring to this it is worth studying the formula which the letter writers use to put together a good, publishable letter. These serious papers often print quite long letters which deal with matters of a political or economic nature, with several aspects of a particular subject being under discussion.

Other national "dailies", such as *The Daily Mail* or *The Daily Express* carry letters which concern all manner of topical subjects. These letters tend to be shorter than those carried by the more serious papers, and generally deal with one point only, as this is usually all that space will allow.

By far the easiest place to get a letter to the editor published is in your local newspapers. Letters vary in length and are usually concerned with local issues about which many people feel very strongly.

When writing a letter to any newspaper it is worth remembering the following points.

(a) Always type your letter in double line spacing.
(b) Choose a subject that is topical and about which people will be interested to read.
(c) Be as concise as possible. Don't let your letter "stray to other irrelevant points, or its impact will be lost.
(d) Establish beyond doubt that your facts are absolutely correct and that you are not writing anything of a libellous nature (see Chapter 4).
(e) Before sending your letter, be completely sure in your own mind that you are prepared for it to be published. Remember, that in receiving your letter any editor would rightfully assume your automatic consent to its publication.

I have not included any examples of these letters in this book, as I believe that studying the letters in the various newspapers is by far the best way to learn what is required.

Part 3
Social Letters

11
Starting a Social Letter

Presentation

Below are some useful tips to bear in mind when writing to friends and relatives:

1. Try to write as clearly and neatly as possible. We all like to receive letters and to enjoy the news they contain, but this pleasure is lessened if we have to spend a long time deciphering each word.
2. If you are writing to old people or to youngsters, don't write too small. Both groups will be able to read larger writing more quickly. Children also love the occasional drawing, even if you are a poor artist!
3. Quite a few people, especially those who do not write many letters, forget to insert the date, but I feel it is important to date *all* correspondence. Even on personal letters, it gives the reader a reference – especially if you use phrases like "last Saturday" or "next Wednesday".

Setting out Your Social Letters

This section deals with the totally hand-written letter, i.e. one which is not written on printed notepaper.

Generally speaking, I would not type a letter to a friend, I would always try to hand-write it. I would also indent my paragraphs. If you *have* to type a social letter (for instance if the letter is a very long one), I would apologise for the fact that it is typed, as some people could be slightly offended to receive a typed social letter.

When writing to friends, I would usually just put my own address, followed by the date, in the top right-hand corner, and would not bother including my friend's address. I do not normally include my telephone number on letters of this kind unless I need an urgent response.

An example of this type of heading is as follows:

The Green House,
Tiverton Road,
SWINDON,
Wilts.
SN3 4PP

(the date)

One point worth noting in this heading is that the name of the house is not in inverted commas. Many people used to (and still do) put the name of the house in inverted commas. It is not necessary to do this unless the name is a quotation, although it would be a good idea if the name of the house also happened to be that of a town, as below:

"Tavistock",
Sandy Lane,
READING,
Berks.
RG2 7AC

The alternative style of heading is the centred one, like the one above.

Opening and Closing

The opening is correctly called the *salutation* and is the "Dear..." part of your letter, and the ending is called the *complimentary closing* and is the "Yours..." part.

Most people have a telephone so, for instance, if you wanted to make arrangements to meet someone for lunch, or to fix up a game of squash, you are probably more likely to call than to write them a note.

However, a great many people still write letters to friends and relatives on their birthdays and at Christmas, or correspond with people living abroad, and it is useful to know how to start letters in these circumstances.

I always feel that when writing social letters, informality is the rule. But how you start your letter usually depends on how well you know the person to whom you are writing. Below are a few ideas for you to use as a guide when beginning your letters.

To a Parent/Parents

Usually, you would start with "Dear Mum/Dad", or "Dear Mum and Dad"; or, in speech, you may call them "Mummy" and "Daddy", in which case you may start "Dear Mummy and Daddy". I would think that rarely, nowadays, do people call their parents "Mother and Father", but if this were the case, again, you could begin "Dear Mother and Father".

If you are very close to your parents, you may wish to begin with the word "Dearest...".

A friend of mine called her mum by a "pet" name, which was "Poppet"! When writing to her, or sending her a greetings cards, she may have put "Dear Poppet". It would be quite OK to start your letter in this way if you call your parent/parents by an endearing "pet" name.

To Grandparents or Brothers/Sisters

When writing to grandparents or to brothers/sisters, the same rules would apply as when writing to parents (see above).

To Aunts/Uncles

Just start, "Dear Auntie Pam", or "Dear Uncle John"; this should be correct. You may begin with "Dearest" instead of "Dear" if you are very close to your relative. This would also apply to unrelated older family friends whom you may call "Auntie" or "Uncle" in speech, but who are not, in fact, related.

To "The Other Half" (e.g. Wife/Husband, Engaged Couples, Boyfriend/Girlfriend)
Again, "Dear Steve/Jackie" is usual, but some may wish to begin with, "My darling Steve/Jackie", or possibly just "Darling". I feel that romantic beginnings are probably more likely to be put into greetings cards than into letters.

Many couples have silly "pet" names for each other and they may start with, "Dear... *(followed by the "pet" name)*". You only have to look at the Valentine's Day greetings in newspapers to see the fantastic names couples dream up for each other!

Close Friends
Here again, "Dear James" would be correct. However, you may like to begin with "My Dear James". Or, if you prefer, you could start "Dearest Sue".

Adults to Their Children
"Dear Pippa" or "Dear Jamie" would be usual; although you may wish to start with "Dearest". The same would apply when writing to nieces or nephews. Again, it would be acceptable to start with a "pet" name.

Youngsters to Youngsters
When youngsters are writing to each other "Dear Phil/Jan" would almost certainly be used.

Youngsters to Adults
When writing to an unrelated older person, you would generally use the same style as you would if writing to an aunt or uncle.

Youngsters would probably put "Dear Mr/Mrs Brown", unless the person they were addressing was, say, an old unrelated family friend whom they called "Auntie/Uncle".

If the youngster was on first-name terms with the adult to whom he/she was writing, they could put "Dear Mike/Jane".

The general rule is that anyone with whom you are not on first name terms should be addressed as "Dear Mr/Mrs", that is unless they have a title or are a doctor or clergyman. For Forms of Address And Subscription see page 30.

Closing a Letter to all the Above Groups
There are several ways in which you could close letters to the above, any of which would be suitable depending on your relationship to the person being addressed.

Suitable endings are: "Love"; "With much love"; "With all my love"; "With my love and very best wishes"; "With very best wishes". All these should be followed by your first name.

When adults are writing to adult acquaintances, they might just sign off with "Yours", followed by their name.

If an elderly aunt were writing to a youngster she may sign off "Yours affectionately".

Signing Off

Generally, I would not print or type my name at the bottom of a letter to a friend or relative, as I would expect the recipient to know who had sent it. However, when signing off a letter to people you do not know very well, it is always a good idea to print your name in capitals underneath your signature so that they will know to whom they should reply.

Numbering Your Pages

When writing a letter of more than two pages, it is always sensible to number the pages so that your recipient has no difficulty in reading it. You do not have to start each page on a fresh sheet; it is acceptable to write on both sides of the paper.

There is no real need to number your first page, as it will be obvious, from the top of it that this is where your letter begins. Page 2 can be written on the back of the first page, then page 3 on a new page, with page 4 on the back of it, and so on.

Keeping Copies Of Correspondence

I would not generally keep copies of letters to friends.

However, if you only write to someone once a year (at Christmas, for example) it might be a good idea to keep a copy of the letter so you can remember what you said last time!

The Technique of the Longer Letter

Many people find the writing of a long letter a very difficult matter. However, the most important thing which the beginner has to learn is that a letter, to be really effective, should be written more or less as one would speak. In other words, do not sit down, look at the paper and think: "Oh dear, what can I *write?*", but just begin writing the letter as if you were talking to the person. In this way your letter will really come alive.

Another point to be remembered is that if you put yourself in the place of the recipient and try to think of the things he would like to find in the letter, you will get ideas as to what to write.

In long letters, try to avoid putting in extra words just for the sake of length, otherwise the letter is apt to be boring. Also remember that it greatly adds to the interest if you can quote what friends have said, or tell of a humorous happening to yourself or someone else. Human interest is generally more exciting than anything else.

Another factor creating a good letter is the avoidance of too much about the obvious. Fill your letter with as much unusual information as possible, particularly with material which you know will be of especial interest to the person receiving the letter.

12
Thanks and Things

"Thank You" Letters

The "Thank You" letter is probably one of the easiest to write, because it is always easy to express gratitude.

The only problems that you might encounter are that your letter may not sound very sincere, or that it may appear too 'gushing'; what you should try to achieve is something between the two! The other problem is that you may find your letter is not long enough. It doesn't have to be a great long screed, but it shouldn't be too short or it could appear merely businesslike. If I am faced with this problem, I get round it by writing the "thank you" part in the first couple of paragraphs, then I extend the letter with another couple of paragraphs of news (i.e. what I've been doing, etc.).

Christmas or Birthday Gift

One of the most common needs for a thank you letter is for a birthday or Christmas gift:

Dear Mum and Dad,

You shouldn't have! But how lovely that you did! I know we've already said thanks on the phone, but I just wanted to write, and again say thank you so very much for your wonderful present.

Imagine, a week in Paris! You'll never know how delighted Jane and I were when we opened the envelope on Christmas morning and found the two tickets inside. It was such a fantastic surprise!

How kind of you to think of it; you know how much we've been wanting a break, but with all our outgoings at the moment, a holiday just was totally out of the question.

Anyway, now that we've got our breath back, you must come over soon for the weekend. I'll call you next week so that we can fix up a date.

With all our love and thanks,

Wedding Presents

Another common occasion when a thank you letter is appropriate is for wedding presents. You can buy special cards for this occasion which are blank inside for your special message. As you will probably have quite a few people to write and thank, it is best to keep each note on the short side; if you write a long letter to each one, you'll be at it for days! The following gives you an idea of the type of information you could include:

Dear Auntie Pat and Uncle Stephen,

Thank you both so much for the beautiful duvet and linen set you gave Bob and me as a wedding present. They are already being put to good use, and look absolutely lovely in the bedroom now that we've finished decorating.

Our honeymoon in Rome was wonderful. Although I'm not sure we did everything the Romans do! The sun shone, and we both came back with a smashing tan. It really was the holiday of a lifetime. What a way to start married life!

However, we're back down to earth with a bump now and are surrounded by pots of paint, as we continue to do up the house. It's a labour of love, though, and everything is really starting to take shape.

Hope you are both keeping well and that we will see you again very soon.

With our love and best wishes,

Occasional Presents

Sometimes, you may be given a surprise gift "out of the blue" and although you would probably phone to say "thanks", there may be occasions when you feel that you would like to send a note. Here is an example:

Dear Paul and Sarah,

Sorry we missed you when you called, and how kind of you to bring us so many lovely plums from your tree. When we arrived home and saw the box on the doorstep, we wondered what on earth could be in it. When we saw all that fruit we were worried that you may not have kept enough for yourselves.

Oh, but they're *so* delicious. We've eaten lots of them already and Sally's in the kitchen at the moment making pies for the freezer, as well as freezing most of the remaining fruit so that I don't eat it all now!

It was a lovely thought and much appreciated, and I hope we'll be able to return the favour when our rhubarb crop comes up next year.

With our very best wishes and thanks,

Service Rendered

If someone does you a good turn it is more than likely that you will want to write them a letter of thanks. The following example is from a grateful patient who has just come out of hospital.

Dear Dr. Scott,

Now that I'm home and settled back in, I just had to write and thank you for making my stay in hospital such a comfortable one.

The dedication of you and your team, and the kindness of the sisters and nurses on Beauchamp Ward were unequalled. Your professionalism and efficiency were always evident and served as a great boost of confidence to all the patients.

With my grateful thanks and very best wishes to you all,

Thanks after being Entertained

If you are invited for a meal or to stay for the weekend with friends, they will more than likely go to a lot of trouble on your behalf. It is therefore good manners (and will be appreciated) if you write a note of thanks. You could write something like:

Dear Mike and Caroline,

Just a quick note to say how very much we enjoyed our weekend with you; thanks so much for inviting us. The break did us the power of good, and what with the delicious home cooking and excellent company – well – we could have stayed forever!

Our journey home was very pleasant. We stopped off in the New Forest for a cream tea on our way back, and arrived here at about six o'clock.

Once again, many thanks for your hospitality and hope to see you both very soon.

With our love and best wishes,

Letters to Children

As I advised earlier, always try to write as simply and clearly as possible. Children always want facts to the bitter end, and are not interested in possibilities and probabilities. Never leave an incident unfinished, and try also to keep the style of your letter very simple and easy to understand. For small children write as neatly as possible, and leave a gap between each letter, as it will be much easier for them to read.

The following are two letters which you could use as a guide if you have to write to children. The first is a thank you letter for a Christmas present:

Dear Peter,

Thank you so much for the lovely plant you got me for Christmas. I have put it on my table by the window and it looks really pretty.

Did you get lots of presents at Christmas? I know you were hoping to get some "Space Giants", and I hope you did.

We had a lovely surprise on Christmas morning when our cat, Blackie, had six kittens. They are still very small, but will soon be running about. Your mum has said that she will bring you over to see them on Saturday, so we will look forward to seeing you then.

With lots of love,

The next example of a letter to a child is one wishing a little girl "Get Well".

Dear Jane,

I saw your dad in the supermarket tonight and he said that

you were in bed poorly with mumps.

How horrible for you! I remember when I had it. But not to worry, you will soon be up and about, and you will have a nice few days off school while you get better.

John said he would like to cycle over to see you on Saturday, after Scouts. He had mumps last year so he will not be able to catch it again, and he would very much like to come round and cheer you up a bit.

We all hope you will soon be feeling much better.

Lots of love,

Sending a Gift

If you send a gift to someone, it is always a good idea to send a little note with it. (Otherwise, your friend may not realise who sent the present!) Such a letter could say:

Dear Christine,

I went up to London yesterday and was browsing round one of the big music stores there when I came across the enclosed CD and just *had* to get it for you.

Isn't it a coincidence that only the other day we were talking about it and the problems you've had trying to get hold of a copy? I do hope you enjoy it.

Let me know if you want any other of his albums (they had a very wide selection), as I'll be going up there again next Monday.

With love and best wishes,

Greetings

If you are sending, for example, a Christmas card to friends overseas, you may feel that this alone is insufficient and that you would like to include a little note. The following is an example of the sort of thing you could write.

Dear Barry and Lyn,

Just a quick note to let you know we all remember and think about you both.

Hope you are still enjoying yourselves out there and we are all looking forward to seeing you when you come over for a holiday in the Summer. Things here are quite hectic in the run up to Christmas, so I will keep this note short and write you a long letter in the New Year to let you know what we've been up to.

Hope you all have a smashing Christmas, and we wish you every happiness in *date*.

With our love and best wishes,

13
Good Luck and Congratulations

Here, again, are two subjects which make letter writing an enjoyable experience, and most of us will have to write such a letter at some time. I am always pleased to be able to wish friends "Good Luck" with their exams or when starting a new venture, or to be able to say "Congratulations" to them for some special achievement.

There are special cards which you can buy for these occasions and you could use one of these in which to write your note if you prefer.

Letters to Wish "Good Luck"

It is always nice to be able to wish someone "Good Luck", and there are many times when we can do just that. Some of the most usual ones follow.

New Job

One of the most frequent "Good Luck" letters is one to wish a colleague all the very best in a new job, and I begin by giving an example of this type of letter.

Dear Sarah,

I never really got a proper chance last night at your leaving celebrations to wish you the best of luck in your new job. We'll all miss you at Broxham's – life just won't be the same without you!

But less of my whingeing! I truly hope that this new job will give you every opportunity to progress in sales – an area which I know you've not really been able to develop at Broxham's. From what you told me, it seems like just the right step for you, and I know you'll make a great success of it.

Do keep in touch and let me know how you're getting on. Maybe we could meet for a drink or lunch in a few weeks' time, when you're settled in? 'Til then...

Love and very best wishes,

Friends Starting Their Own Business

With an increasing number of people now becoming self-employed, I thought it would be useful to include a letter of good luck to someone starting a new business. The following example is to a couple who have just set up their own small hotel.

Dear Roger and Vicki,

You made it! Well done! I just had to write and wish you every success with your new venture.

All the hard work must seem really worth it, now that you see what a beautiful place you've created for your guests. I remember coming over to you at Orchard Farm last Spring and thinking how brave you were embarking on such a task! All that renovation and conversion...! (Do your guests know they're sleeping in what used to be the cow byre!?!)

I was pleased to hear that you've already got a lot of bookings, and I'm sure that once those people go back and tell all their friends what a good time they've had, your business will continue to go from strength to strength.

If you can find the time, do drop me a line in a few weeks to let me know how you're progressing.

All the very best,

Emigrating
There may be a time when you wish to write a good luck note to someone who is going abroad. My example letter is written to friends who are only going to be abroad for a couple of years; but it could easily be adapted for friends who are emigrating permanently.

Dear Jan,

Many thanks for your letter; Peter and I were so surprised to hear your news. It's wonderful that David's company is giving him the chance to work in the States for two years – what a marvellous opportunity for you both. But it's all happened so quickly; you can hardly know whether you're coming or going!

I think you're wise not to sell the house, and it's nice that you're letting it to someone you know.

What's your house like in New England? I hear it's a beautiful part of America, and I'm sure you'll love every minute of it.

By the time you get this letter you'll just about have your suitcases packed, and I'm sorry that it wasn't possible for us to travel down to say a personal "Goodbye". Peter and I just want to wish you and David all the very best of luck, enjoy yourselves, and please keep in touch.

With lots of love,

Entering a Competition
This could apply to many things: scout badges, ballet exams, beauty contests, fishing competitions, etc. The recipient of the following example letter is planning to enter his home-grown produce in the local country show and his niece is writing him a letter to wish him luck.

Dear Uncle Alan,

I was so sorry to have missed you when you called last night. Mum told me all about you entering your vegetables in next week's Uffcombe Show, and I just wanted to drop you a line to wish you good luck.

We all know how very hard you've worked in your garden this year, and if anyone deserves first prizes for everything – it's you!

I will be going to the Show, so will make a point of going straight to the Produce marquee to see how many rosettes and cups you've won! If you'll still be around at three o'clock, maybe you'd like to meet me at the tea tent for a celebration cuppa.

'Til then, we all wish you the very best of luck, and we're keeping our fingers crossed for you (not that you'll need it!).

With love and best wishes,

Letters to Say "Congratulations"

There are many occasions when we like to give our friends a handwritten "pat-on-the-back", and some of the most common examples are given.

Passing Exams

Dear Tracy,

Uncle Adrian and I were so pleased to hear that you passed your City & Guilds Hairdressing exams and that you've found a good job at a top London salon. You must be absolutely delighted. Our warmest congratulations to you.

Your mum tells me that after you've had a few years'

work experience you hope to open your own salon. I think that's a wonderful idea; there's nothing like being your own boss. All the hard work and headaches are worth it, believe me!

Anyway, very well done, and hope to see you soon.

With our love and best wishes,

Job Promotion

Dear Richard,

I was delighted to hear about your promotion. Congratulations! I heard the news from Robert last night when we met for a game of squash.

You really do deserve this step up the ladder; I've often wondered when your company would recognise your talents, and now they have. Not before time, though!

This new direction will give you a lot of scope for developing your style, and I'm sure you'll soon be making your presence felt.

Well done – and all the very best.

Yours,

Driving Test Pass

Dear Pete,

Well done mate! I bumped into your sister in the High Street today, and she told me you passed your driving test the other week.

Have you got yourself a car yet? I know you had your eye on that little Golf down at Green's Garage; will you be able to buy it now – or have you done so already?! If I know you, I'll bet you were straight down there, even before the ink had dried on your test pass certificate!

It's such a long time since I saw you. Let's get together soon – maybe a trip down to the coast would be good for a laugh. We could go in my car and share the driving if you like? Let me know.

Well, congrats. again, and hope to see you soon.

All the best,

New Baby

Dear Laura,

Congratulations! Rob phoned us this morning with your wonderful news. A baby girl – you must be delighted; I know that you both secretly wanted a little girl.

Rob sounded absolutely ecstatic when he rang! He gave us the complete run-down of the proceedings and was so thrilled to have been involved at the actual birth. We were pleased to hear that you'd had not too difficult a time, and that you and little Maxine (love the name) are progressing well.

If it's O.K., we'll pop down to see you once you're settled back at home.

'Til then, take care of yourself – and Maxine!

With all our love and very best wishes,

14
Sending and Replying to Invitations

Informal Invitations

Invitations, particularly to parties, are becoming less and less formal, and often nowadays, people will make up their own funny invitation, or they may buy special invitation cards or pads; or they may phone. I personally think that just relying on the telephone is not such a good idea, as people are apt to forget the date. It is better if they have something in writing, and you may feel that a short note would be best. I have given below three example invitations for different occasions.

Invitation for a Weekend Stay

Dear Mark and Angie,

Now that we have (at long last!) finished renovating our house, we wondered if you would like to come down and stay with us for a weekend next month. It's been so long since we've seen you, but as you know, it was just not possible for us to invite anyone when the house was in such a state.

It would be lovely to show you the area too. There are lots of delightful 'olde worlde' country pubs with real ale and home-cooked food, and there are several National Trust properties close by which we know you'd enjoy visiting.

We're busy the first weekend, but please drop us a line and let us know which of the other weekends would suit you, and we can take it from there.

Look forward to seeing you soon.

With our very best wishes,

Invitation to a House-Warming Party

Dear *(name to be filled in by hand),*

As you know, we have just had a very moving experience!

...and our new address is:

15, Herrington Crescent,
LONDON.
SW12 5TY
Tel: 0171-600-0098

We're having a bit of a knees-up Saturday 14th March to celebrate the move and to toast the new house, and would be delighted if you could join us. We'll be kicking off at about 9.00 p.m. and hope to see you then.

With best wishes,

Invitation to a Surprise Party

Dear *(name to be filled in by hand),*

On 26th March, Philip will reach the ripe old age of 40!

To celebrate the fact, I'm arranging a **SURPRISE PARTY** for him at The Doves Restaurant, Henley Street,

Banbury, on 26th March, and would love it if you could come along. There will be a buffet supper and drinks laid on, as well as dance music. If you are able to come, please can you arrive by 7.45 p.m. sharp, as I'll be arriving with Philip at about 8.00 p.m., and would like to have everyone there before us.

At the moment, Philip thinks that he and I are just going to the restaurant for a quiet candlelit dinner (won't he be disappointed!!) and I would really like to keep it that way – so if you see him please don't breathe a word.

Please let me know if you can come. I would be grateful if you could reply to the address above (which is our neighbour's address), as I obviously can't have any replies arriving at home!

Hope to see you on the 26th.

With best wishes,

To save you writing out several invitations, just do one (either typed or hand-written), have it photocopied, then fill in the names – it's much quicker!

Replying to Informal Invitations

It is a very easy matter to reply to informal invitations, but I will give an example of an acceptance and a refusal which you may like to use as a guide.

Acceptance

Dear Carol,

Thank you so much for your kind invitation to the surprise party you are holding for Philip. We would be delighted to come. What a lovely idea; I can't wait to see his face when we all spring out of the woodwork!

As you know, Roger is seeing Philip for a round of golf on the same day, but don't worry; I have primed him not to mention it.

Look forward to seeing you at The Doves next month.

With our very best wishes and thanks,

Refusal

A letter of refusal is probably a little more difficult to write, as you do not want to offend anyone. If you have a previous engagement it is quite acceptable to refuse because of it, but I think it is courteous if you can say what the previous engagement is. All you need to do is write a short, simple, friendly letter, and leave it at that. An example could be:

Dear Mark and Sue,

Thank you so much for your invitation to the house-warming party, but I'm afraid we won't be able to make it as we have already made arrangements to spend the weekend with Caroline's sister in Dorset.

We'll be sorry to miss the party – your 'gatherings' are always such great fun! – but I hope that we can get together very soon. Hope you all have a good time on the 14th.

With our very best wishes and thanks,

Formal Invitations

These are very useful when a large number of invitations need to be sent out. Also, for a more grand occasion – a wedding, for instance – a printed formal invitation undoubtedly looks better.

Cards can be purchased which are either specially

printed or bought for the purpose at a stationer's. The quality of the invitation will obviously depend on how much you want to spend. Both the ready-bought ones and the specially printed cards will usually come with their own special envelopes.

A wedding is probably the most common occasion when a formal invitation card would be used, and I give below an example of the wording of such an invitation.

Mr. and Mrs. Dennis Clark
request the pleasure of the company of

....

at the marriage of their daughter
Caroline Angela
with
Mr. Simon Charles Swinton
at St. Matthew's Parish Church
Harrington Road, Bath
on Saturday, 18th May, XXXX
at 2.30 p.m.
and afterwards at
The Seagrove Hotel, Middle Street, Bath

3, Mere Close,
BATH,
Avon.
BA3 4HG   R.S.V.P.

Everyone knows R.S.V.P. means "Please Reply" and comes from the French phrase, "Repondez s'il vous plaît".

Replying to Formal Invitations

When replying to such an invitation, you should do so as soon as you receive it. There are special acceptance/

refusal cards for wedding invitations, so you may prefer to send one of these instead of writing a letter. These are widely available from stationery shops.

If, however, you do want to send a note, it should be written on good quality notepaper. Make your answer as brief as possible, and, strictly speaking, it is correct to reply in the third person. A suitable formal reply to the above invitation would be:

Mr. and Mrs. Peter Mitchell thank Mr. and Mrs. Dennis Clark for their kind invitation to their daughter's wedding at St. Matthew's Church on Saturday, 18th May, XXXX and to a reception afterwards at The Seagrove Hotel, and are most happy to accept
(or, if you cannot attend)
regret that they will not be able to attend as they have accepted a previous engagement on that day.

This note should not be signed.

However, just because a formal invitation has been sent does not necessarily mean that you must send back a formal reply. Some people feel that a reply such as this is unnecessarily formal, especially if you know the people to whom you are writing. So you could write something like:

Dear Mr. and Mrs. Clark,

Thank you so much for your kind invitation to Caroline and Simon's wedding on Saturday, 18th May, and to the reception afterwards. Stuart and I would be delighted to attend and look forward to meeting you on that day.

Yours sincerely,

(sign your name in the usual way)

If you are unable to attend you could make the final sentence:

Unfortunately, Stuart and I will be on holiday that week, so we regret very much that we will be unable to attend.

Whichever style you choose, the main thing to remember is to be courteous and you will not go far wrong.

15
Love Letters

Perhaps in no field of letter writing are the opportunities for achievement greater. Between those who are in love, or between two people, one of whom is in love with the other, the letter can provide an opportunity for expression which would not be possible otherwise.

However, despite that, I would avoid being too passionate and 'flowery'. Although you might talk this way when you are together, I feel that such things are intensified when set down on paper. This is particularly so if you are writing to someone you do not know very well. In this cynical day and age, there is the danger that a passionate letter could appear grossly insincere, or even, in some unfortunate cases, be an object of ridicule. So be careful what you write. By all means let your loved one know you miss him (her), but don't be too elaborate about it; and do include other, more general, information in your letter which would be found interesting.

There is also one warning which might be worth noting about being too passionate in ink, and this is that there is always a danger of the letters getting into the hands of someone for whom they were not intended. One regularly sees this sort of thing being reported in the press as having happened to someone of note, and it is a sad fact that some unscrupulous people do have such a blatant disregard for the privacy of others. Don't think because you are just an ordinary person that it couldn't happen to you – it could; especially if you are involved in a risky or clandestine relationship.

You should always try to avoid writing and sending letters in the heat of the moment – either after a quarrel, or perhaps because you are a victim of unrequited love. At some later stage you may really regret having posted it.

However, if you do write such a letter, keep it overnight and don't mail it until you have read it again the next day. If it is still appropriate, send it by all means, but you will most likely be glad that you didn't!

Another reason why you should choose your words carefully is that they could easily be misunderstood by the recipient – either by giving the impression that you are more interested than you really are; or by your not appearing to be interested enough.

There are many instances when you would write a letter to a loved one, and in the following I have tried to include some of the most common examples.

Married Couple – One Working Away From Home

It is not uncommon for lovers or married couples to be separated by hundreds of miles, and in these cases phoning every day may not be possible so they will have to keep in touch by post. These letters are fairly straightforward, and in a case where there is mutual understanding there should be no danger of anything written being misunderstood. These letters, therefore, can be long, and filled with material which will be interesting to the recipient.

My example letter comes from a wife whose husband is working away from home for a short while.

Dear Jon,

Well, here I am! Hope you're O.K. and having a good time – well not *too* good!

I went down to see my Mum and Dad on Saturday, and Mum and I spent a lovely day looking round all the shops – I didn't spend *too much* money! It was great; I managed to get all my Christmas shopping done. I can't believe how organised I am this year – you ought to go away just before Christmas *every* year! No, I didn't mean it!!

On Saturday evening I took Mum and Dad out for a bar

meal to The Red Lion – you know, the little place at Cherringbury. The food was excellent. I stayed the night at my parents' rather than driving all the way back here.

I got home at about 10 o'clock on Sunday morning, and no sooner had I come through the door than *your* Mum phoned! She and your Dad popped over in the afternoon and ended up staying for dinner – we had a lovely time; it was nice to see them both.

So – what I thought was going to be a dismal weekend turned into a mad social whirl! I still missed you, though. I'd forgotten how lonely it can be – even when you're with family and friends.

I've been really busy at the office. That new project we've been working on is now in its final throes, so uncontrolled hysteria has broken out to get it finished on time. I've not been working too late though; in fact I've been getting home early enough to do a bit more decorating. I've finished painting all the woodwork in the hallway and dining room and I thought I'd do the hallway ceiling tonight if I've got time.

Oh, guess what? You remember I applied for tickets for us to see that new show in the West End? Well they arrived today and we've got fantastic seats – only two rows from the front. I can't wait!

You'll never guess what I've been roped into doing by our mad next door neighbours. I've said I'll go carol singing with them next week! I must have been asleep or something when I agreed to it! It should be a good laugh; about twenty of us are going round the town next Tuesday and Wednesday evenings; and it's all for a good cause – the church organ fund, I think. Peter and Julie have invited me to have a meal with them before we go out, so that'll be nice. Everyone's been really great – phoning and calling round to make sure I'm O.K. It's lovely of them to bother isn't it?

How are things with you? Hope your meetings are going well. Have you had chance to do any sightseeing yet? If so, what happened to my postcard?! I'm sure the next couple of weeks will go by quickly enough but it seems like an eternity 'til you come home. The old saying "Absence makes the heart grow fonder" is so true, but I could do without the "absence" to make me realise it.

Anyway, I'm writing this in my lunch break which is just about finished, so I'd better go and get back to the mass hysteria...! If you have time, drop me a line and let me know how you're getting on. It really won't be long before you're back, so 'til then, take care.

All my love,

Holiday Romances

Quite often, people will meet on holiday and may wish to write to each other when they return home. Here again they may be separated by many miles, which always puts extra strain on any relationship. However, their correspondence could help the friendship develop, but they must be cautious about what they write, as one of them could easily get the wrong idea about the other's feelings.

The following example is written by a young man who has met a girl on holiday and whom he hopes to meet for dinner in a few weeks' time.

Dear Jackie,

Hope you arrived home safely and that the train journey wasn't too long and boring! It only took me half an hour to get back; after I'd found my car in the airport car park, that is! I spent ages looking for it and was beginning to think it had been stolen; but no, there it was, asleep in a quiet corner!

Although it's only been ten days since I got back, the holiday seems an age away. It's amazing how quickly you slip back into the old routine, isn't it? But it's nice to remember all the good times we had – all those lovely warm nights down at La Costa drinking gallons of sangria, then staggering back along the beach to the hotel...

How's your work? Have you been busy? What have you been doing with yourself? Is there much to do up there; what sorts of places do you go out to? You must drop me a line and let me know how you're getting on.

Work has been keeping me very busy since I got back. We have an exhibition coming up at the end of next month, so I'm working hard putting all that together. It's my job to design the stand and make sure that all the things we want to take will fit on to it; and I'm pleased to say they do. It's looking really great – even though I do say so myself!

In fact, the exhibition is one of the reasons why I'm writing (apart from obviously wanting to find out how you are). By an amazing stroke of luck, the exhibition is being held in Manchester, and I will have to come up there for a few days when it is being assembled. As it's only about 20 miles away from where you are, I was wondering if we could meet for dinner or something while I'm up there?

I would really love to see you again, and hope that you'll be able to make time to meet me. I'll be in Manchester from the 20th of next month until the 25th. Let me know if any of those dates are good for you, then we can take it from there.

Look forward to hearing from you soon,

Girlfriend/Boyfriend at Different Universities

One of the most common forms of romantic separation is when one or both of a young couple goes away to college or university. These are especially difficult relationships to maintain because the two begin to make completely new lives for themselves and may end up growing apart. They will be meeting new people all the time, and will normally lead much more liberated and independent lives than when they lived at home. This can be very distressing if one drifts away but the other remains as romantically attached as before, and it is a sad fact that this type of relationship can often end in heartbreak.

The following example is written by a girl who has just moved away to one university and is writing to her boyfriend who has started at another.

Dear Tim,

Just thought I'd write you a quick letter to let you know how things are going here and to see how you're getting on.

I arrived at the halls of residence at about six o'clock on Saturday; my dad brought me down because I had a lot of stuff to bring. My room here is quite cosy and the halls are in a nice part of town. All the girls along my corridor are really friendly and have asked me to go out for a drink with them on Friday to the Union bar. There's a band on too, I think, so it should be quite good. Have you been out much? What are your digs like; is the landlady a "dragon"?

It's all so strange still – I've not really settled in properly yet. It's just so different from living at home. I really do miss you *so* much. When do you think you'll be able to come over for a visit? Try and come next weekend if you can. There's a good group on at the University, that you'd like.

Our lectures started today and all our tutors seem very pleasant. It's so nice – they actually treat you like adults – not like at school! We have quite a lot of work to do apart from the lectures, so I've made a point of disciplining myself to make sure I get all the work done. The university has a brilliant library where we can go and study, so I'm down there most days.

How's it all going with you? What's your course like, and the tutors, and the college – everything? Write and let me know how you're getting on. Have you made many friends yet – hope there aren't any attractive females there!

Anyway, I'd better go now. Lisa from next door has just popped her head round to see if I'm going down to dinner with her.

Write soon, won't you, and try to come down next weekend if you can.

Miss you...

All my love,

Breaking off a Relationship

Unfortunately, there are times when writing a letter to a partner can be an extremely difficult matter. The most obvious occasion which springs to mind is when breaking off a relationship. Normally it is best to deal with this unpleasant and often emotionally painful situation face-to-face. However, some people feel that they can express their feelings better in writing, and prefer to send a letter to their partner for fear of being misunderstood if they discuss the matter in person.

The following example is a letter from a man who has been living with his fiancée, but has just walked out on her because he feels he cannot go through with the marriage.

Dear Jenny,

I realise that leaving like this and writing you a letter must seem like a total cop-out, but I just know I'd not be able to find the right words – or the courage – if you were here. I've no doubt that after you've read this you'll want to talk, and so do I, but I felt it would be easier – for both of us – if, first of all, I just took my things and went, and explained my reasons here in this letter.

The thing is, Jen, I just can't go through with the wedding. I've thought and thought about everything so much, and I've reached the agonising conclusion that our marriage just won't work. If we're honest with ourselves, the relationship's been on rocky ground for quite a while now, so what's it going to be like if we get married? It's so easy to let things just drift on and on, and I think one of our biggest faults has been the total lack of communication between us. Maybe we were hoping that by some miracle everything would just get better; but we can't sweep our problems under the carpet any longer.

Now that I've done this, I feel I must be totally blunt and honest with you. The plain fact is, Jen, that I'm really not in love with you enough to spend the rest of my life with you. For me, the problems began when we started living together; I just don't think we're well suited, either physically or emotionally, and there's no point in trying to make a situation work which is obviously not meant to be.

I just want you to know that there's no-one else, and never has been, and that it's breaking my heart having to do this to you. You're a really terrific person, and I hope there will be some way in which we can still be friends after this awful time in our lives has passed.

I will be staying at my brother's for a while and will be there if you want to call me.

Talk to you soon,

(The writer of this letter would probably then just sign his name. Neither "Love" nor "Best wishes" as a closing line would really be appropriate.)

16

Bad News, Apologies, and Get Well Messages

Bad News

Being the bearer of bad tidings is never an easy task, but it is often less distressing to put unfortunate news in a letter than it is to tell it to people face-to-face.

News of an Impending Divorce

The first example letter deals with the unhappy situation where a wife is writing to a friend to say that her husband has asked her for a divorce.

Dear Rachel,

Rather than you hearing my unhappy news second-hand, I want you to know that after thirty four years of marriage my beloved Jeremy has asked me for a divorce in order to marry his mistress. Under the unpleasant circumstances I have had to agree; this has caused both me and the children deep distress.

At present my future is very uncertain; however, I am living at the above address until the end of February. I hope that you will keep in touch as I have always valued your friendship.

Yours,

Child Killed in an Accident

The next example of a "bad news" letter is where a father is writing to friends to say that his daughter has been killed in a road accident. News of this nature would be particularly distressing to convey in person and I would imagine that people would find it much easier to write.

Dear Andrew and Margaret,

I am so sorry to have to write to you like this but I just couldn't find the courage to telephone you with our devastating news.

I'm afraid that Joyce and I will have to cancel our stay with you next weekend, as Janice was killed in a road accident on Saturday evening. You may have seen the reports about the pile-up in fog on the M25; well Janice was one of the drivers involved.

As you can imagine, Joyce and I are absolutely distraught, but we are fortunate that Mike and Sarah have been able to get back here, now, as we all share the worst of our grief.

The funeral is being held on Friday and after that we will be trying to pick up the pieces and get on with life. If I may, I will be in touch in a little while to arrange another visit which I'm sure, then, will be just what we need.

With our best wishes to you both.

Yours,

Apologies

Here again, people may find it is easier to send a note of apology than to say a personal "sorry" to someone they have offended. I have given three examples of apology letters which cover quite different subjects.

Speaking out of Turn

Dear Eleanor,

I realise that I'm probably the last person you would expect (or want) to get a letter from, but I have been so worried about yesterday that I just had to write to you.

The first and most important thing I want to say is "Sorry". I can't think what possessed me to be so rude and thoughtless. My only excuse (and it's a pretty pathetic one!) is that I was having a really bad day yesterday, and when you called with your problem it was just the straw that broke the proverbial camel's back and I just lashed out. But that is no excuse, and my behaviour was totally unacceptable and uncalled for, and completely unforgiveable.

I know I should have thought of it yesterday before I opened my big mouth, but I really would be very sorry if this incident totally ruined our friendship – even though you would be perfectly justified in never speaking to me again. I don't want to go on and on, but I just really hope that you will be able to accept my apology.

Please call me if you feel you can.

With my sincerest best wishes,

Accidentally Hurting Someone's Dog

The next letter is one to someone whom the writer does not know and deals with an accident involving the stranger's dog.

Dear Mr. Jackson,

I just wanted to write and say how sorry I am for knocking

your dog, Tara, over yesterday. I know you have taken her to the vet and that the injury to her leg is not serious, but I still feel absolutely dreadful.

You have been so good about the whole thing, and I know that there was nothing I could have done to avoid the accident. But, having a dog of my own, I can appreciate how upsetting it is when something like this happens.

I'm so glad Tara will be O.K., and although you said yesterday that you wouldn't dream of letting me give you anything towards her vet's bill, I feel it is the least I can do, so I would be very pleased if you would accept the enclosed cheque which should at least cover some of the cost.

Thanks again for being so understanding, and I hope Tara makes a full recovery very soon.

With my best wishes,

Unable to Keep An Appointment

If you are unable to keep an appointment, for whatever reason, it is always a nice idea to write a short note of apology, as in the next example.

Dear Katherine,

I just wanted to write you a quick note to apologise for not being able to keep our theatre date last night.

It's just typical, isn't it! We book up weeks and weeks in advance and what happens – I go and get the 'flu and miss what was, I'm sure, a truly unforgettable evening.

I was so relieved you managed to get Michelle to go with you at such short notice; I would never have forgiven myself if you had gone on your own, or missed it altogether. Did she enjoy the show? Please give me a call when you have a minute, and tell me all about it.

With love and best wishes,

"Get Well" Messages

One is always concerned when learning that a friend or relative is unwell, so it is nice to be able to send them a get well greeting. There are special cards for this purpose which can be bought from most stationery shops. You could buy one of these cards and write a little note inside; however, it would be just as much appreciated if you wrote a letter on a good sheet of notepaper.

Below are some different examples of "Get Well" messages.

"Get Well" Message to a Friend

The following letter is a straightforward message to a friend to say "Get Well".

Dear Alison,

I saw David in town today and he told me you're laid up with a bad back. How awful for you. A slipped disc is such a painful thing; I remember when I had one a couple of years ago, I was in agony. Has the doctor said how long you'll be out of action?

I just wanted to say "Get Well Soon" and I hope that this little card will cheer you up a bit. Maybe I could pop over for a cup of tea and a natter one evening? I'll call in a day or two to see when would be a good time.

Hope you'll soon be feeling much better.

Lots of love,

Sending "Get Well" Greetings via Someone Else

A variation of a "Get Well" message is writing to the partner or relative of someone who is ill so that they can pass on greetings for you.

Dear Mary,

I was so sorry to hear that Dennis has been taken into hospital, and I just wanted to write this little note to ask you to pass on our best wishes to him for a speedy recovery.

If you need a lift up to the hospital or into town, Gordon and I will be only too pleased to help, and if there's anything at all that you need you only have to ask.

Once again, our fondest get well greetings to Dennis for a speedy recovery, and our very best wishes to you.

Love,

17

Letters of Sympathy

These are probably the most difficult of all letters that you will ever have to write; although there are some people who have a gift for them.

In past years, when writing letters of condolence following a bereavement, it was customary to write a lengthy letter dealing with certain aspects of the deceased's life and perhaps mentioning such matters as his long association with this or that, but generally the message of sympathy is apt to be lost in words describing matters which are usually very obvious to the recipient, and therefore unnecessary. In such instances, a simple sincere message usually meets the case best.

Even if you are well acquainted with the person to whom you are writing, it is always difficult to convey true sincerity without sounding gloomy or dramatic. My advice would be to keep sympathy letters fairly short and not try to write too much. Care is also necessary in case any double meaning is accidentally conveyed, and it is also very easy to sound extremely tactless in these letters – so beware! One thing to remember is that there is usually something positive in any unfortunate situation, and it is a good idea to try and be as optimistic as possible when writing letters of sympathy.

Although bereavement is the most obvious occasion when you would write a sympathy letter, it is by no means the only one. Many instances require a letter of this kind – from a house fire to exam failure.

However, as bereavement is the most common, I will deal with this first, and the following examples cover a variety of different condolence letters. In the first three, the letter writers are assumed to be quite good friends of the people to whom they are writing; the others are from someone who is only an acquaintance.

Parent Died

Dear Jane,

I was so sorry to hear the sad news about your Mum. It seems like only yesterday that you and I were coming in from school and she was giving us cheese on toast and those delicious home-made cakes.

She was always so good to me, and I will really miss her. I can only begin to imagine what a terrible time this must be for you and your family. I will, of course, be coming *(to the funeral)* on Friday and will see you then, but if you need *anything* in the meantime, please don't hesitate to call, will you?

Please send my condolences to your Dad and to Neil.

Love,

Child Died

Dear Sue and Steve,

I saw Eileen today who told me of your dreadful loss, and I just wanted you both to know that Vicki and I are thinking of you all at this terrible time. How is little Sarah taking it? It must be a comfort having her there with you.

I realise that at this moment you must be feeling utterly wretched, but I hope it may help you to know that the same thing happened to my sister, Helen, three years ago, when she lost her little boy through cot death. After her heartbreaking experience she started up a support group for parents like yourselves, and she has given hope and comfort to a great many people over the last couple of years. I know it's still early days yet, but if you feel you would like to give her a call, either now or in the future, I know she would be pleased to hear from you. Her number is Stubbington 8996875.

I do hope this may be of some help and that we will see you soon under happier circumstances.

With our love and best wishes,

Baby Stillborn

Dear Janet,

I met Peter in the supermarket tonight and he broke your sad news to me. I'm sure I can't even pretend to know how devastated you must feel, but I was relieved to learn that the doctors say you will have no long-lasting physical effects and that it was a chance in a million that this tragedy happened. Even so, that must seem like small comfort at the moment.

Peter says you are coping well, and if I know you, I'm sure that's true. With your down-to-earth approach to life and your strength and determination, I know you'll be able to put this unhappy time behind you.

If you'd like me to call round for an evening I'd love to come, but if you'd rather not, I understand perfectly. Just let me know.

With all my love and best wishes,

Husband Died Tragically

Dear Mrs. McLeod,

I was stunned to read the report in today's local paper of Alan's dreadful accident. How awful for you to lose him so tragically. The suddenness of such a loss is particularly upsetting, and the unfairness of losing one so young can never be fully understood.

My husband, John, and I just wanted you to know that our thoughts are with you and the family at this sad time. Alan was always such a cheerful person and so helpful when he called, and I know he will be sorely missed by many people in the town.

We do hope you will be able to find the courage to pick up the pieces and carry on, and we wish you everything that is good for the future.

With our kindest regards.

Yours sincerely,

Death of Wife

Dear Mr. Robinson,

I have just heard with profound regret of your wife's death after a long illness. As you know, my wife and I enjoyed her friendship and hospitality on so many occasions that we feel her passing in a very personal sense and well understand how greatly you will miss her. You have our deepest sympathy.

Yours very sincerely,

Death of Business Associate

Dear Mr Black

We were distressed to read the announcement of Mr Pollard's death in this morning's "Times", and write immediately to express our deep regret. By his untimely passing the computer industry has lost one of its pioneers. We recall his many kindnesses to our firm in the past, and we appreciate how much he will be missed by all who knew him and particularly by your numerous employees. He was a great man.

Yours very sincerely
KERR, BROWN & SONS LIMITED

Jonathan Jones
Director

The following are examples of sympathy letters for all kinds of occasions.

Exam Failure

Dear Graham,

I was sorry to hear from your Mum that you won't be going to medical school next year. You must be so disappointed; Uncle Alan and I know how much becoming a doctor has always meant to you.

Your Mum tells me you will try again next year and that you have got a job, in the meantime, at the local hospital. I know you will enjoy it, and it'll be very good experience for you. You never know, in a few years' time you might be glad you didn't get into medical school this term!

Both Uncle Alan and I wish you every happiness in your new job, and every success when you take your exams again.

I do hope we'll see you in the not-too-distant future.

With all our love,

Failed Business

Dear Jeff,

I was so sorry to hear that your business venture didn't work out, and after all the hard work and effort you put in, too. What a blow. If anybody deserved to succeed, you did. It was just your luck that as soon as you started trading the lending rates went sky-high and the economy headed for a recession. So many small businesses are going the same way, and it's a tragedy to see all the hope and optimism turn into misery and despair. Anyway, at least you can say you "had a go" which is more than most of us can.

But I just know you'll bounce back from this, and I hear that you're already fixed up with a job; I hope all goes well.

Look forward to seeing you soon.

With my very best wishes,

House Fire

Dear Terry and Jean,

We were very sorry to hear about the fire; what a terrible thing to happen to you so soon after setting up home.

I am also writing to let you know that we have a spare bed and a dining suite stored away doing nothing in our loft, and we would be delighted to lend them to you 'til you get sorted out. They're not great to look at, but will do the job until you can get something more suitable.

If you are O.K. and don't need these, don't bother to get in touch as I know you will have a lot on your minds at present. But please don't hesitate to give us a call if you'd like the furniture; it would be no trouble to drop it round.

Hope things are soon looking brighter for you.

With very best wishes,

Burglary

Dear Ted,

We were so sorry to hear the terrible news that you had a break-in last week. It must have been dreadful to come back and find the house in such a state. At least they didn't take anything of sentimental value – I suppose that's something. Is Betsy still very upset? Having a burglary is one of Christine's biggest dreads. It's such an awful thing I just don't think she could cope if it happened to us.

The positive thing you mentioned in your letter is the fact that the police seem to have a good idea who is responsible. Have they managed to catch him yet?

I do hope that you will both be able to put this terrible incident behind you. Now that you have made your house more secure, I'm sure you must feel a lot happier.

Please give our love to Betsy, and we hope to see you both very soon.

With best wishes,

Made Redundant

Dear Sam,

It was nice to see you again today, but I was very sorry to learn that your company has been taken over and that you have been made redundant. It must be very sad for you after all these years; I know how much you enjoyed your job. You'd think that if you worked for a company for as long as you have they'd show a bit more respect; to be given just three days' notice is a disgrace. I suppose the one good thing is that at least your redundancy payment should be quite good.

So, what will you do now? Have you any plans? It would be nice to hear what you have in mind; I didn't really get a chance to chat about it today. Maybe it's time you and Betty moved down to the coast and started that little guest house you've always dreamed about? In a few years' time you'll probably look back and see this redundancy as a godsend!

Do keep in touch, won't you, and let me know how you're doing.

All the very best to you and to Betty,

Business Colleague – Accident or Illness

Dear Mr Fulmer

I was very sorry to hear, when I called at your office today, that you had been in the Rugby to London train accident, but equally relieved to learn that you are now making satisfactory progress and will be about again in a month's time.

In a long talk with your Manager I was told business is

good and your firm has received a large number of orders for your new project. I shall be seeing him again next week and hope to hear that you are much better.

I expect to be in Northampton in a fortnight's time and hope to come and see you.

With kindest regards.

Yours sincerely

In many such instances, of course, one would use the Christian name. It is a custom I prefer, provided people know and like each other well.

Part 4
Business Letters

18
Techniques

Dictation to a Secretary

Dictation is a pleasant way of dealing with correspondence and may give a better flow to your style. Some people find dictation difficult, but practice should help. Start with short, easy letters, and as your confidence grows, try dictating longer letters. It would help to make a list of the important points you wish to mention, in the order in which you want to present them. This should avoid omissions. It is boring for a secretary to wait for someone to gather his thoughts together, who then makes stabs at what he wants to say, only to change his mind. Sudden, galloping dictation is just as difficult. Secretaries prefer to work for somebody who dictates fluently and clearly.

A newly-qualified college leaver has learned the theory but has yet to gain the practical experience which a job will give her. She will need time to get used to the routine, and the new people. It is important to try to put her at her ease. She may have to learn some specialised terms which apply to your particular trade or profession, and in the first few weeks she may be rather slow and possibly inaccurate. Dictate steadily, so that she can keep up with you. As her confidence builds up, her skills will improve too. Many secretaries would like the opportunity to use their own initiative. Inexperienced secretaries could start by answering queries or dealing with routine letters. Experienced secretaries will be able to answer many letters, and deal with most situations that might arise in their employer's absence. Both will need to learn your particular way of answering correspondence.

Dictating Machines

For letters, there is no substitute for a good secretary. She can remember when you last wrote to Mr Smith, or quickly recap on the dictation when it has been interrupted by a telephone call. The tape or cassette can be rewound, but it takes longer.

However, nowadays most companies use dictating machines and have a pool of audio typists sharing the work which has previously been fed into tape recorders.

When dictating for audio typing, you must give all the information *first,* i.e. which type style to use (where applicable), which paper, etc. Any mistakes made during the dictation should be erased from the tape and re-dictated.

Although I feel this is an impersonal method of working, it does have many advantages. A busy person can use a tape recorder whilst travelling to and from work, or on business trips. Also, if a typist is ill, letters can be transcribed at a later date, or by somebody else. In addition, a typist can get on with other work while letters, etc. are being put onto the machine.

Finally, don't forget to thank your secretary when she has done well. Respect her intelligence and so far as possible try to use the full extent of her abilities. This is rarely easy because so much office work (indeed any work) is repetitive and tends to be dull. If she is good, look after her.

It's the art of keeping what, in another area, is called a "happy ship" that is so important; sadly that's not always easy.

The Word Processor

Whether a word processor is right for your business depends on the type of documents that form most of your typing work. The most common and effective uses of the word processing system are for repetitive work such as standard letters, mailing lists, legal documents, records, proposals, manuals and reports where sections of the text of one document can be stored in the memory and slotted into the appropriate sections in different documents. This avoids the constant retyping of practically identical or identical copy. It will also speed up day-to-day ordinary correspondence in that it may make corrections easier.

The word processor allows the printing of many perfect copies with minor changes such as a different address, name, final sentence, etc., in a fraction of the time it would take using a normal typewriter.

Word Processing on Computers

If you do not have enough suitable work to justify a word processor full time, one of the many word processing packages available for computers would be a solution. You would be able to combine other facilities with it, such as your accounts, invoicing and stock control.

Using the Word Processor

Standard Letters

From reminder letters on overdue accounts to personalised mailing shots for advertising or marketing – all can be done quickly and efficiently on a word processor. The standard part of the text of the letter is printed out and the system automatically merges the names and addresses, which you have stored in the machine, and inserts these at appropriate points in the text.

Reports and Legal Documents

The first draft is typed into the word processor, stored in the machine and a copy is printed out for the author to correct. Only the corrections need to be typed in again. The remaining text is untouched and so does not have to be retyped. New sections or paragraphs can be inserted and existing text refined or deleted. A high-quality result is achieved remarkably quickly.

Brochures and Price Lists
It is a simple task to update all kinds of business literature including mailing lists and manuals using a word processor. Only the changes will need to be retyped.

The Printer

A printing device is essential, as there is no point in saving and editing text only to look at it on your screen. Choose your printer with the utmost care and attention. A wrong choice could lead to a frustratingly slow volume of work and may perhaps not have the capability of printing the graphics or kind of typeface you require.

The Fax Machine

Sometimes your letters or messages may need urgent communication and you may need to send a fax.

Efficient Faxing

The following are guidelines for efficient faxing.

Numbering the Pages
Write or type the message on a photocopy of the organisation's letterhead or a special fax form and indicate the total number of pages being sent by stating 'sheet one of four', 'sheet two of four' and so on.

Legal Documents
Unique documents, and any legal documents, should be duplicated by a top copy sent by post. Faxing is essentially a photographic process, and there is the possibility that the print will degrade in time.

Confirm Receipt
Don't assume that a fax sent is a fax received. If the message is urgent, telephone to confirm receipt, or ask for confirmation by return fax.

Confidentiality
Remember that faxes are not usually confidential.

Overseas Correspondence

Business letters to overseas correspondents must possess the same qualities as those intended for home "consumption", though they may require greater *expertise*. There are several points to remember.

First, the recipient is several hundred miles away, and if your letter is not clearly expressed he will be faced with difficulties which he cannot immediately clear up. He may have to telephone or fax you to clarify the matter.

Secondly, there is the difficulty of language. Even though your correspondent may be in an English-speaking country, always use *plain* English and avoid slang terms or any words which are not in common use. The chances of being misunderstood are otherwise intensified. In Britain, for example, we call an "apartment" a "flat", and "pants" are described as "trousers". Unfortunately, both these words mean entirely different things in America! In that country, for instance, sweets are called "candy", and biscuits "crackers".

Ideally, of course, men and women handling foreign mail should have lived for some time in the country concerned, or at least have visited it, so that they can appreciate the finer points of custom and usage, but a possible substitute is to read books and magazines published in that country so that your own approach becomes less insular and acquires the right "slant".

Fundamentally, foreign mail is dealt with in much the same way as home correspondence, but letters which may take weeks to reach their destination must be written with that fact in mind. Letters which are to be sent by air mail can be written on very thin paper, or, of course, the air mail letter form, so that the weight is reduced to a minimum.

Letters going to places with unfamiliar alphabets (e.g. China, Japan, Greece, Russia, and Arab countries) should have the envelopes typed in CAPITALS, or written in block capitals.

Replying to Letters

It is best to follow an organised method of dealing with

your correspondence. One satisfactory way of answering a letter is to make pencilled marginal notes of any points which occur to you as you read it quickly through the first time. It can then be re-read more slowly and additional notes made. The reply should be dictated to a secretary or dictation machine or typed straight on to your typewriter/word processor (if you do your own typing), or, of course, handwritten, and, as the letter is composed, a pencilled line should be drawn through the original letter, *marking off each paragraph as it is dealt with. When the line passes completely through the text, you can be reasonably sure that no section of the letter has been overlooked.* Ensure you are not one of the many people – perhaps the majority – who deal with two or three points and forget the rest, or go off at a tangent and omit to answer several important matters.

See page 33 for further points about replying promptly and efficiently to letters.

Do not forget that every reply costs money. A business friend of mine has computed the amount per letter to be frightening. It is often feasible to include other material in your reply. This point should receive careful attention, because on many occasions answering a letter provides an opportunity for the introduction of some new and possibly profitable subject, or the inclusion of a leaflet of a new product.

From what has been said, it should not be inferred that if you get silly questions asked in your mail, you are obliged to reply to them. There are a few people who write for catalogues, particulars and technical information rather for the fun of the thing and, if encouraged by lengthy and explanatory replies, might end up by absorbing all your time. In such cases, some of the points may have to be ignored and a short reply sent as a matter of courtesy.

It is a good idea to send a postcard acknowledging receipt of correspondence if a lengthy and complicated reply is essential. This is not only courteous but allows you more time to compose your reply.

19

Style and Stationery

Letter Headings

These should contain the name of the company or organisation, its place of registration, registered number and the address of its registered office (if different from the heading), directors' names, the postcode, telephone number(s), telegraphic address and telex and fax numbers.

Styles of Letter Headings

A business with wide contacts with the public, or with many new customers, benefits by creating a good first impression. Many firms like to use a colophon or logo, which can look attractive on the notepaper, and you may choose to do this.

Letter headings may also be die-stamped or embossed, but as these methods cost more, most companies now use a cheaper style and forgo the elegance for economy. Some people like a simple basic style of heading which gives the impression of dependability, whilst others prefer a more modern design. Remember to choose a style which will suit you and your profession or trade; a loud letter head would hardly do for a consultant surgeon.

A few firms use advertising matter in their letter headings and there is no special reason against this. Some firms might have a photograph of one of their products or of their shop or factory. Another firm might wish to put line drawings of several of their products, perhaps down the side of their letter heading. Again, many might wish to give a list of their products. All this, however, is somewhat beyond the scope of our book, except to say that unless it is very well done it can look a mess. So if you are going in for this type of advertising on your letter heading, be sure to ask your printer's cooperation in the layout. If he has not got an art department it may mean employing a local advertising agent or studio. The point to remember is that these people can be very expensive so it is wise to enquire about the cost first.

One important point to bear in mind is to choose a type style that is easy to read and not too small (especially for telephone numbers). It is better if letter headings are not printed smaller than "10 point" capital type (to the layman that means the letter should be a minimum of just under 3mm/ 1/8 in deep) as then all the important information can be obtained at a glance.

For appearance and economy of space however, the heading should not occupy more than approximately 5cm/2 in of an A4 page, otherwise insufficient space is left for the letter itself. Frequently about 2.5cm/1 in is enough, whilst for half-sheets 2cm/3/4 in may suffice. Also, if the name and address occupy a centralised position, less space is sacrificed – an important consideration for half or small sheets of notepaper.

I personally prefer to see commas used to separate the different parts of an address on headed notepaper as I think this makes the address easier to read. For example, if the address was 222 Downs Way North Newington, it would not be clear (particularly to a foreigner) whether the correct address was 222 Downs Way, North Newington, or 222 Downs Way North, Newington.

Coloured inks can be used either on the letter heading or for the contents, but black is still frequently used.

Some firms, such as mail order businesses, find that when they make a major alteration in the layout of their headings, or change the colours and design, this attracts new business, and is therefore worth the extra cost. It is only fair to add that in many trades it probably makes no difference.

A business may be well advised to include in its letter heading the statement: "Goods offered subject to prior sale and confirmation", as this affords some protection against errors in quotations.

The layout for letter headings can, as a rule, safely be left to an experienced printer unless you have any preference, which should be indicated in your copy or verbally. He should be requested to use a clear, bold type, and submit proofs for your approval on the paper to be used for the job.

Stationery

Notepaper

For suitable sizes of notepaper it will be found that general business needs are met by the metric international size A4 sheets (210mm x 297mm/8¼ in x 11¾ in) and A5 sheets (148mm x 210mm/5⅞ in x 8¼ in).

A common and good practice is to include a square or oblong for the reference. This brings the reference to notice and, suitably placed, acts as a guide to the typist in setting the margin, giving the letter a balanced, neat effect.

Similarly, a special space can be set aside for the recipient's address. This is often the practice when the letter is to be sent in a window envelope. The corners of the space can be marked as a guide for the typist or the whole space can be enclosed by a box.

A stock of continuation sheets, headed only by the firm's name and the word "Continuation", can be carried if any long letters are anticipated, or plain paper can be used instead, but one usually finds that most letters can be typed on a single page.

In large organisations where different departments need a copy of any relevant correspondence, sheets of varying colours may be used for the different copies. But in smaller companies, plain white paper is quite acceptable.

Chairmen of large companies often have their own special notepaper and heading; when this is done, it is normal to use an expensive paper, often a grey or blue tinted paper. Any good printer can advise on this.

For firms doing overseas business, a supply of specially thin and light-weight air mail letter headings may be required. A neatly printed air letter heading is much more attractive and imposing than the old-fashioned method of stamping your firm's name and address onto the paper.

Envelopes

The type and size of envelopes used are a matter of taste, although metric-sized envelopes are generally used to match metric-sized paper. Some wealthy organisations will have tinted notepaper and envelopes to match; others may have definite views about the size of their envelopes; they may, for instance, prefer the square to the oblong size for general use.

It is also a useful precaution to have all envelopes stamped or printed with the sender's name and address on the flap, or, for larger envelopes, on the left-hand corner of the face. This is naturally of assistance to the Post Office – and may also serve the additional purpose of dissuading employees from using business stationery for their personal correspondence.

It helps the Post Office if you use the Post Office Preferred (P.O.P.) range of envelopes and cards. To fall within the P.O.P. range, envelopes should be at least 90mm x 140mm and not larger than 120mm x 235mm.

Acknowledgements

If yours is a business which is of small or medium size, acknowledgements can be sent on an ordinary A5 letter heading, but if you have a business which receives many letters it would pay you to have either:

(a) Postcards already printed with wording such as:

"Dear Sir(s) or Madam,

I/We thank you for your letter of........................
and hope to reply fully in a few days."

Or (b) An A5 letter already printed, on similar lines to (a) above.

Or (c) Instead of having the postcards or letters actually printed, you could type out the basic wording onto appropriate-sized paper or card and use a photocopier to produce the required number of copies, or keep it in the memory of a word processor.

With staff costs soaring and competition severe, it is usually wise to make use of the latest office equipment to produce these time-saving methods.

Of course if your business requires only the occasional copy of some document you will not need to have a photocopying machine on your own premises. Instead it will be cheaper for you just to visit one of the many shops in our high streets which provide such a photocopying service.

Office Forms

One can save an enormous amount of time and therefore money by having systems worked out to meet recurring conditions. Many successful firms have been doing this for years.

Standard forms can be used for giving quotations to customers, for example:

Thank you for your enquiry of.................... We have much pleasure in quoting as follows:

....

....

They can also be used for advice notes, with wording perhaps like this:

Our representative, Mr John W Hall, will have much pleasure in calling upon you at .... a.m. on ....

The following form is one which happens to be applicable to our business.

Your trade or industry will require different wordings and while one does not want to go "form mad", by thinking and planning you can save much time and effort. We have worked out forms for contracts, placing orders and enquiries as well as a mass of office forms.

It is usually impossible to depend on the required forms to be found in the shops, as the wording rarely fits in with individual needs.

As with the acknowledgements, these forms can either be printed specially or photocopied when required, with the relevant figures, dates, etc. being filled in, and/or the appropriate boxes being crossed or ticked where applicable. Another alternative is to store the basic information and layout in the memory of a word processor/computer and just print out the sections which apply to the particular correspondent.

Preparing your own forms as required is certainly time well spent.

Name: .... Thank you for your order. Please return this form with your reply to save delay.

Address: ....

....

The item marked [x] is applicable to you.

☐ This book is out-of-print so is no longer available.

☐ Your letter contained no money. Perhaps you overlooked it. The envelope was shut. Please send cheque/postal order and we will despatch.

☐ The book(s) you enquired about is/are available. Please send cheque/postal order and we will despatch.

☐ We do not accept credit cards since we are not retailers.

☐ Your cheque is not negotiable because it is unsigned/out-of-date/words disagree with figures. Please correct, initialling any alteration, or send a new cheque, and we will despatch.

☐ You do not say which book(s) you require, please give details.

Memoranda

These forms are used for inter-office communication. They are often headed as follows:

MEMORANDUM

FROM:	REF:
TO:	DATE:

SUBJECT:

The text is then typed without further preamble.

Digests and Précis

A digest merely means a summary and is often drawn up for the benefit of busy executives or officials who have not the time to devote to reading through long texts or reports. Although its importance lies in its being short, nothing of value must be omitted; niceties of style and all extraneous matter must be eliminated for word economy, so that the reader is in possession of all the salient facts and sufficient of the original text or report to enable him to grasp it thoroughly.

A *précis* is a French word meaning "summary" or "abstract".

20
Simple Business Letters

By simple letters I am referring to letters which deal with comparatively unimportant subjects; this leads to the statement that many letters should never be written at all. Letters are sometimes sent to enclose invoices and statements, cheques, catalogues and so forth. The businessman will do well to remember that a letter costs a lot more than the stamp. There is the time involved, the paper and other materials used; every business should do its best to cut down *superfluous* paperwork. This does not mean, however, that letter writing should be limited to those which are absolutely essential; the question of courtesy and the value of having copies of correspondence must be considered.

For example, a firm may have asked other firms for quotations to supply some stationery, and as a result may have received six quotations. It will not be necessary to acknowledge each quotation. On the other hand, for a shipbuilding firm which has solicited quotations for specifications in steel or timber, possibly running into hundreds of items, it would only be polite to acknowledge the quotations in appreciation of the immense amount of work which will have been done by the estimating departments of the possible suppliers. Such matters are really only questions of common sense.

Setting out Your Business Letters

As for official letters the first things you should put on the letter are your address and company's name (if you are not using printed notepaper), the recipient's name and address and the date. The full name and address of the recipient should always be included as it will appear on your copy of the letter and you will then have a reference for further correspondence. Similarly the date is important so that expected or overdue replies can be checked against your copies.

Copies

In many cases, copies of simple letters are unnecessary and merely a waste of time. In some large concerns, copies of *all* correspondence may be essential, not only for filing purposes but to advise other departments of action already taken. However with small firms and one-man businesses a vast amount of time and paper can be saved by writing on the original letter the word "acknowledged" and the date and any other explanatory remarks necessary.

Copies of all important letters must, however, be retained for future reference, and, of course, they would be required in any legal proceedings. If a typist is employed, the dictator of the letter must, therefore, remember to mention which letters require copies being made.

Example Letters

Here are some examples of simple letters:

Dear Sirs

<u>Re: Order No. 9654</u>

In reply to your letter of 20 May XXXX we are pleased to advise you that the goods will be delivered to your warehouse on 15 June XXXX.

Yours faithfully
COOK & FISHER LIMITED

J A Cook
Manager

Dear Mr Carter

Mr Smith has asked me to acknowledge your postcard of yesterday's date and to say that we hope to call upon you on Monday next, 25 September XXXX, at 4 p.m.

If this suggested time is inconvenient to you, please telephone to let us know; if we do not hear from you we shall assume our proposed arrangement stands.

Yours sincerely
HOWARD & HOWARD LIMITED

S K French

Dear Sir

In reply to your enquiry of 2 August XXXX, regarding the price of the Denton-Mullet fax machine, this retails at £xxxx (plus VAT). We would be pleased to give you a demonstration should you care to call on us at our showrooms at the above address.

Yours faithfully
SUPER BUSINESS MACHINES LIMITED

A T Smith
Sales Manager

Dear Sirs

Thank you for your enquiry of 12 May XXXX. We will send you a quotation within a few days.

Yours faithfully
COURT & KING LIMITED

A B Burke
Manager

Dear Mr Chalfont

Thank you for your letter of 1 February XXXX.

I am carrying out some research into the question you raise and will write to you again in a few days' time.

Yours sincerely
CASH & CARTWRIGHT LIMITED

A S Newman

Dear Mr Blackburn

Very many thanks for the telephone message which I received this morning. The information will be extremely useful to our Public Relations Department.

Yours sincerely
CASH & CARTWRIGHT LIMITED

A W C Wittering

As stated at the beginning of this chapter, there is no need to enclose a letter with an invoice, or cheque, etc. This also usually applies when sending small gifts at Christmas, such as calendars or diaries. In most cases, a compliments slip would suffice. There are, however, occasions – especially when dealing with good customers – when Christmas cards or calendars may be sent with personal letters; alternatively, personal letters alone may be preferred. The following is a simple letter which would be appropriate in such an event:

Dear Mr Aitcheson

I am writing to wish you and all the members of your firm a very happy Christmas and good fortune in the coming year.

The co-operation which you have extended to us during these most difficult times has been greatly appreciated; it is to be hoped that the future will be easier for us all.

With kind regards.

Yours sincerely
FITZGERALD & SMITH LIMITED

James Fitzgerald
Managing Director

It is a general rule never to write letters unless they are necessary; keep simple letters clear, short and courteous.

21

Letters to Officials

A letter to a government department or civil servant should, of course, be quite a straightforward matter. Once it is despatched, you must be prepared to possess your soul in patience, for replies are often slow in coming.

Such letters may concern taxation, permits, licences, permissions and so forth. Some people seem to be much more successful in their dealings with authorities than others. Why is that? I think the answer is that the successful ones know more about how to approach the official mind. They marshall their facts in a way that appeals to bureaucratic instinct and tend to express their views in a factual and non-emotive way.

They display patience, persistence, courtesy, firmness and diplomacy, also sometimes flattery.

In this chapter, I give three examples of the sort of letter that you may sometimes have to write to officials. The first one concerns a planning application to build an office block right outside my office window. The neighbour has applied for planning permission, and I am exercising my right to object to the application by writing to the Chief Planning Officer.

Planning Application No: 89/PO550
Re: Application by Messrs Jones, Jones & Smith to build a 3 storey office at 47 London Road, Walton Vale, Surrey. Objection from The Little Company.

Dear Sir

1. Location
The premises of The Little Company are shown on the site

plan edged green, with the buildings edged blue. The applicant's site is edged yellow, with the proposed new office-block shown coloured pink.

2. Use of Buildings by The Little Company

The existing buildings have windows on the south side at ground floor level only. These windows are of the offices used both for general office work and for proof-reading which is work requiring particularly good lighting. Two photographs are attached. The photograph marked (a) on the back shows exactly where the wall of the office-block would be in relation to our office window. This photograph is taken from point (a) on the plan. As will be seen, the office-block will take a large percentage of the light from the particular windows.

The photograph marked (b) is taken from point (b) on the plan, and shows the position of our windows in relation to the boundary line. In the event of planning permission being granted, we would have no alternative but to bring court proceedings for an injunction to restrain the erection of such a building by reason of its effect on our established rights of light. The legal advice we have received is that such an injunction would be granted.

3. Our Submission

Although we have our private legal remedies in respect of loss of light to our buildings, the consideration set out above is a material consideration for planning purposes, as confirmed by several recent court decisions. We therefore ask that full weight be given to this point in the determination of the application.

We urge that your authority should refuse permission for the development which has been proposed, and we look forward to receiving from you, in due course, notification of the Council's decision.

Yours faithfully

Planning departments generally treat reasonable local objections very sympathetically and such a letter would have a good chance of preventing a development which might otherwise easily be allowed.

The second example is a letter to the tax authorities in respect of someone whose tax code is wrong, and who is therefore suffering deduction of income tax when this should not be happening.

THE KING'S HEAD
North Road
Ewell, Surrey
KT20 1AB

1 March XXXX

The Inspector of Taxes
Ewell 3 District
London Street North
Cardiff
CF2 8UP

Dear Sir

Re: Miss J Masters,
Her National Insurance No. is ZZ111111Z

Miss Masters works for us as a part-time barmaid on Friday nights and Saturday and Sunday lunchtimes only, and earns less than £XXX per week. She is in fact still a university student; she does not do any other work, and she has signed a statement to that effect on form P46 which we sent to you when she commenced employment two months ago.

Despite this, you have coded her on code 0, week one basis, and this means that we have to deduct income tax from her pay with no allowances at all.

Miss Masters informs us that she has complained to you on three separate occasions about this mis-coding, but she has never even received the courtesy of a reply. We are in the difficult position of being required by law to deduct tax on the basis of the code number which you have supplied for her, although we are well aware that she should not be suffering this tax deduction; in fact she is entitled now to a considerable refund.

Will you please therefore, as a matter of urgency, provide us with the correct code for Miss Masters, as a school-leaver in a first job with no other income. If your reply with the correct code is not received within the next seven days, we shall assist Miss Masters in taking the matter up with our local Member of Parliament.

Yours faithfully

In the case of civil servants who are totally unreasonable or incompetent, it is often found that a threat to place the matter in the hands of the local Member of Parliament will bring about a swift resolution of the problem.

The next letter concerns a staff member of otherwise good conduct who has unfortunately become embroiled in a fight outside the local pub in which someone was quite seriously injured. The young lad has been found guilty of Assault and will be sentenced after reports from the Social Services, Probation Officer, etc., have been taken into consideration. Since this person is a good employee who has never caused any problem at work, you wish to try to help him and could write to the Court as follows, addressing your letter to the Clerk to the Justices.

Dear Sir

We have been asked to write to you concerning the character of Mr John Smith who, we understand, has been found guilty of Assault.

Mr Smith has worked for us for the last three years, ever since leaving school, and his duties include photography, plate-making and colour-origination for the printing industry.

We have found him to be a valuable and conscientious worker, and he is paid at the top rates for an apprentice of his age.

Mr Smith has a good job here and is highly regarded by all his colleagues. If he were to be sent to prison, he would lose the opportunity of securing a really good qualification in the printing industry and the excellent career that could follow for a man of his ability. If he were sent to prison, he could in fact very well become embarked upon a lifetime of crime, to the detriment of both himself and of society at large.

The circumstances of his conviction have been explained to us, and I must say that we find the story to be totally out of character with the John Smith that we know here. We feel sure that this aberrant behaviour results only from some uncharacteristic over-indulgence following his sister's engagement party.

While we are not in any way seeking to condone the seriousness of the crime that has been committed, we would nevertheless urge that in these particular circumstances the matter would be best dealt with by non-custodial means.

Yours faithfully

22
Important Letters

I must begin this chapter with a strong warning. When you have an important letter to deal with – particularly one that entails a serious decision or a question of policy – do not be in a hurry. Remember, too, that letters can have consequences which may not be foreseen or intended by the sender. Therefore make it a firm rule that you should endeavour to call on the person concerned, if this is at all possible, so that you can talk the matter over. You are then on safer ground. Unfortunately, it is only too easy to be swayed by emotion and prejudice; people do not always approach their problems and difficulties in a scientific and detached way.

Timing

The importance of timing should be mentioned. In writing a policy or sales letter, for example, the date on which it is sent is often an essential factor. Imagine that circumstances have arisen whereby you decide to terminate an exclusive agency. Provided there is no fixed date by which notice must be given, it is obviously wise to wait for the right moment. If the contract involved an exclusive selling arrangement, it would be foolish to send the letter immediately after some large orders had been obtained. Business, goodwill and personal friendship are intermingled in the commercial world to an extent altogether beyond the appreciation of those outside it. To send your letter at such a time would probably create bitterness and justifiable anger, and a great deal of harm might ensue. And, lost goodwill.

On the other hand, if the letter is sent either after a quiet season or following a period during which the business has been bad, the blow will be softened. Do not worry – unless your letter is urgent, it will not suffer by being delayed days, weeks or even (in extreme cases) months. Time often helps to clarify a situation. Naturally, any important decisions will have to be discussed with other partners or directors, and in most trades there are people (perhaps suppliers) of sound judgment who are generally willing to give their advice. Be careful, however, to choose a person whose confidence can be trusted. The advantage of a talk with someone outside the organisation is obvious: he can see the whole matter dispassionately and can bring a completely fresh mind to the subject. Such outside advice may not prove to be correct, but the discussion you have had may enable you to judge the best course to adopt.

More thought should be devoted to the timing of letters than is commonly given.

Prompt answers normally denote efficiency but often an acknowledgement, followed by delay, may be wiser. For instance, in quoting for work, the correct amount of delay could make the difference between getting the order and losing it. A ten-day wait could mean that all your competitors had got their prices in, so that when your representative called with the estimate, he held the advantage that the customer was ready to fix his order. One need not be a genius to be able to judge if one's price is right or too high. At the interview you can often sense if your estimate is out and make a small reduction to secure the order. Sometimes a phone talk before your quotation is sent will gain you valuable knowledge. Nine times in ten the last person to quote, if he is skilful, can get the job or at least the chance of it.

All successful companies pay attention to the timing of sales letters and publicity efforts, often striving to obtain nationwide or worldwide impact by co-ordinating several efforts at once.

Diplomacy

It is always wise for the inexperienced to make a rough draft of their letter first; any omissions or alterations can be made before the final copy is drawn up.

You must try to get the right perspective by putting yourself in the place of the recipient. If you do not want to give him an opportunity to retaliate, be sure to word your letter in such a way that he cannot offer any reasonable argument. Diplomacy is nearly always necessary – for alternatives may exist which will not be altogether pleasant. But what is the secret of this diplomacy? Surely it is the ability to keep something up your sleeve so that you are not obliged to play your last card too early in your negotiations. Remember to avoid any tendency towards discourtesy and appreciate the tremendous power of a polite answer to a discourteous letter.

I give below a few suggestions – with the qualification that they are only suggestions and there will be times when they must be ignored. In exceptional circumstances, drastic action may have to be taken.

1. Never post today what can be posted tomorrow.
2. There is a finality about the written word; respect it. Much can be said over a meal or even at an office meeting which would be unacceptable in a letter.
3. Try to judge the *effect* of your letter upon the recipient.
4. Listen to, but do not necessarily accept, the advice of people of ability and integrity.
5. Worry *before* you post your letter; once you have reached your decision, think no more about it. Remember, however, that having made your decision, you must abide by it and take the consequences.
6. Make your letter absolutely clear. You may have to suffer for it, but there is no point in having to suffer because of a misunderstanding.
7. Avoid words like "ultimatum", "final decision" and so forth; you may have to eat them! If humanly possible, avoid promises at all times, and certainly all forms of threat, some of which may prove to be libellous.

8. There are occasions when letters are a better means of communication than even meetings; for example, they give time for the recipient to consider points.

Problems

It is possible to enumerate all the important matters which may require correspondence, but a few general examples are given below:

Questions of policy frequently cause difficulties. It may be decided, for instance, that the price of a certain model of bicycle will have to be raised substantially. A letter or circular to the trade, informing them bluntly of this advance in price might have a ruinous effect on business. Wherever it is possible to coat the pill with something palatable, do so. Some information might be included on a new advertising policy, the addition of new tools with the machine, or whatever it may be. These extra items may only account for a small percentage of the cost of the bicycle, but the effect of giving the information with the price increase may well reduce the danger of competitors making too much capital out of your altered price.

A seller is sometimes unable to obtain orders from a certain buyer. His firm may feel that the latter is making a mistake in not purchasing his goods and may be tempted to write to the buyer's immediate superior or perhaps to the Managing Director, expressing uncomplimentary views on the buyer's judgment. The latter may be suspected of accepting bribes or of sheer incompetence; but a letter conveying this will not be easy to write, and could be extremely dangerous.

The first point to remember is that most employers have confidence in their staff, otherwise they would probably not retain them. Secondly, your accusations or suspicions may be impossible to prove. On the other hand, you may believe that, although little may be gained, nothing can be lost. An accusation of bribery constitutes a libellous statement and is dealt with in Chapter 4, but a letter informing the buyer's superior that you have found it impossible to sell to his firm's representative is in a different category.

Serious problems can often be overcome in quite a simple way. The difficulty might be solved by saying to the buyer: "Do you mind if I send a sample to your Managing Director? I have a feeling he might disagree with you about the value of our goods." By watching his reaction, you will be able to judge whether or not he is sure of his ground. If all else fails and it is decided to go over his head, try to do so in the least obvious way. The following letter will give some indication of a line which might be adopted. The letter should be marked "Private and Confidential".

Dear Sir

Our representative has been calling regularly in an endeavour to introduce our new "Cut-Clean" Lawn Mower to your company, but we have not so far been able to interest your buyer in the proposition. We have already pointed out that we feel he is making a mistake in not giving this machine a trial, and have also mentioned to him that we would be writing to you as we are sure our machines merit full consideration by you.

The "Cut-Clean" Lawn Mower costs £xxx, which includes delivery to any of your branches, and, confidentially, on an initial order we are prepared to allow you an extra ten per cent discount. Our reason for writing to you is that we did not wish to mention the granting of this discount to your buyer as we are anxious that it should be treated in the strictest confidence.

We hope to hear that we may send you a machine for trial purposes.

Yours faithfully
SMITH & JONES LIMITED

K Smith

Let us take another fairly straightforward example. A UK agent representing an American timber shipper offers you a carload of extra wide Prime Quality Cottonwood. He makes this offer verbally and says he is willing to leave it with you for forty-eight hours. On the second day you telephone to accept the material at that price but the agent informs you he has sold the consignment twenty-four hours previously and has received five dollars more than he quoted you. This is obviously sharp practice, but the agent (presumably as there is nothing in writing) feels legally safe. In certain circumstances he may be, but in this particular case his position is by no means secure. Firstly, extra wide Cottonwood is a rarity; secondly, he has given away certain information – namely, that he sold the wood for five dollars more than he originally quoted you. It is a custom of the timber trade that agents work for a commission, so that, in this instance, the price originally quoted must have been given to him by his principal in America. Your evidence might be based on an offer you had made, by letter, to a provincial buyer. In other words, if you could produce a copy of your offer and a letter from your customer confirming telephone acceptance within forty-eight hours, you would have an almost watertight case. Such a case, however, would be extremely difficult to fight in law and would, of course, require expert and expensive legal advice.

Probably a more effective way would be, firstly, a direct approach to the agent in his office, with a statement that you intend to put the whole matter before his shipper unless he did something about it. As a result, he might give you a letter to the effect that you would receive the next offer of this specification available, in which case you would have won a very good point. If, however, he proved unco-operative, this would afford an excellent opportunity to "go over his head" by writing to his principal, explaining the situation – which would probably get the agent into fairly serious trouble and might even jeopardise his agency. But mark your letters and envelopes "Private and Confidential".

Normally life is too short to go to such a lot of trouble, but circumstances occasionally arise where a stand has to be made – a stand, possibly, largely for the sake of the integrity of the business world – and I have accordingly outlined a suggested course.

Sample letter to American shipper, to fit the circumstances described above, might be as follows:

Dear Sir

Two days ago we received a firm order from your agent for extra wide Prime Cottonwood at $xxx per unit. Your agent made this offer firm for forty-eight hours, and we enclose a copy of our letter to our own customer, Messrs Benjamin Powell & Rankin Ltd, Tenby Road, Liverpool. You are, of course, at liberty to refer to them for confirmation should you so desire. We hold their Order Number 3501 for the goods in question confirming their telephone order.

When we approached your agent well within the forty-eight hours, however, we were informed that the Cottonwood had been sold to a third party at five dollars more than was quoted to us. We regard this as a serious breach of faith on the part of your agent, and as you will appreciate, it has put us in an extremely awkward position with our customer.

We would ask whether you can supply us with another carload of the same specification at as early a date as possible. We much regret having had to write to you direct, but you will understand that there was no other course open to us.

Yours faithfully

A letter couched in these terms is, of course, a very serious matter as the evidence it contains might jeopardise the agent's position. It also contains information which, if it reached the agent's hands, might result in his taking action against you. Such an action would probably be based on a charge of defamation of character on the grounds that the agent had not in fact made you any firm offer. Your customer's confirmatory order, however, would provide circumstantial evidence, and the fact that your letter to the shipper was headed "Private and Confidential" should enable you to enjoy reasonable safety. Before such a letter is posted – and this applies to all similar cases – it is safer to obtain legal advice. But always remember that legal advice *can* be wrong. Personally, I should risk such a letter without fear, if the need arose.

Registration

All vitally important letters should be sent by Registered or Recorded Delivery post, to provide evidence that the letter has been delivered and signed for on receipt. If necessary – certain circumstances may demand this – a spare copy of the registered letter can be dispatched by ordinary post the following day for double safety.

A confirmation of receipt should be watched for by return or within a few posts. Bear in mind that registered letters normally take longer in the post. For next day delivery use the Special Delivery post. Do not register letters that are not of sufficient importance to merit this precaution. In my experience, there are few things so irritating as to open a registered letter only to find it contains information of no consequence.

23

Orders and Confirmatory Letters

Declining Orders

In commerce there are times when, owing to circumstances – weather, perhaps, or sudden runs on stock – orders must be declined because the demand for certain goods exceeds the supply. This situation needs careful handling because you do not want to upset your customers.

A polite acknowledgement of the request should be sent of which the following is an example.

Dear Sir

Thank you very much for the order received this morning for 30 pairs of suede gloves. We much regret, however, that our stock of these particular gloves is now exhausted and it is not expected that further supplies will be available for some weeks. The moment we can let you have a definite order, we will contact you.

Yours faithfully
GREENWOOD & SONS LIMITED

H A Stephenson

If, however, you happen to know of anyone who holds a stock of the goods in question, it is always helpful to give their name and address – a small service which may later be remembered.

A letter declining to fulfil an order because the enquirer's account has not been paid is more difficult. An "Either/Or" ultimatum is almost certain to result in giving offence; something rather more diplomatic is called for. For example:

Dear Sir

Many thanks for sending us your order number 123, but as your account is somewhat overdue and now exceeds £xxxx, we would appreciate a cheque from you before we can enter into further transactions.

We know how difficult conditions are just now, but we have many commitments of our own to meet. If, therefore, you are able to send us a cheque for £xxx in part payment of your account, we shall be most grateful. It will then be possible to supply you with a further quantity of goods.

Yours faithfully
GREENWOOD & SONS LIMITED

H A Stephenson

The wording of this letter will depend upon the decision reached as to how much the customer is to be asked to pay. Remember to mark it "Private and Confidential".

In any refusal to quote, similar courtesy should be shown as it is this sort of thing which builds up the goodwill of a business. It is perhaps hardly necessary to mention that a firm should always quote, if humanly possible (provided there are no financial reasons against this policy), even if it means obtaining a product from a competitor. If such a reputation is once established, general enquiries are more likely to be received.

When quotations are made on behalf of competitors, the profit margin must obviously be small, and unless it is sufficient it will be unwise to incur the risks involved. As I have already stressed, however, it is a sound policy to quote whenever you can.

Judging Integrity by the Letter Heading

It is never safe to judge the standing of a correspondent from the appearance of his letter heading. A dishonest firm may take tremendous trouble with its notepaper; and equally, some perfectly trustworthy businessmen take no trouble whatever. Generally speaking, however, it is true that if a letter heading has been attractively laid out, giving the names of the partners or directors and all other essential information, it is often reasonably safe to assume that the firm is reliable. The information can, of course, be checked if necessary to ensure that it is genuine.

Most firms possess trade directories and lists of customers going back some years. If, for example, the name of a firm appeared two or three years ago and is still on the current lists, that fact should stand in their favour. Sometimes, by judging the quantity of goods asked for in relation to the size of the town or village and *the way the letter is worded,* you can make a reasonably accurate guess as to the integrity of the enquirer. With experience, this becomes almost instinctive.

Dealing with Errors

When an error is detected, it is vital to deal with it immediately. Goods of the wrong size may be delivered, for example, or they may have been damaged in transit; an invoice may have been wrongly charged or calculated. The possibilities of error are unlimited and can only be reduced to the minimum by efficient organisation.

Certain firms have a strict rule that claims must be made within a limited period – seven days, fourteen days, or even by return of post; so act at once. You could telex or fax your claim to your supplier or use the telephone to let him know and then send a written confirmation as well (keeping a copy for your records). These initial letters are not usually difficult to write; it is simply a case of writing to explain the exact position, and the secret of success – if it is a secret – is courtesy and (if need be) firmness. A sample letter in illustration is given:

Dear Sirs

We are enclosing a copy of your invoice for the twelve woollen cardigans charged at £xxx each, which we assume is an error. This sale was made to the undersigned by your representative and the price quoted was £xx for each cardigan.

We shall be pleased if you will confirm this and send the necessary credit note. The goods are of no use to us at the higher price. An early satisfactory reply will enable us to start selling them.

Yours faithfully
W & T BROWN LIMITED

S T Jones
Manager

Do not in any circumstances write as follows:

Dear Sirs

We have your invoice and fail to understand why you have added £xx to the price quoted by your representative. We regard this as extremely sharp practice and shall be glad if you will send a credit note immediately.

Yours faithfully
W & T BROWN LIMITED

S T Jones
Manager

Not only is this a most unlikely way of achieving anything but it is almost sure to result in an answering letter which might lead to trouble varying from insistence that you should keep the goods at the full £xxx to the possibility of legal action. There will in any case be much unpleasant argument.

A good deal of psychology must be used in letter writing. Avoid at all costs this type of letter which comes from a builder to his timber merchant.

Dear Sirs

Your lorry driver delivered 24 boards extra wide oak to our yards this morning. Three of these boards, however, contained large knots, although the wood was understood to be of prime quality when ordered.

We have sent the wood back to you, carriage forward, and return your invoice herewith.

Yours faithfully
JONES & SMITH LIMITED

J Jones

If you put yourself in the timber merchant's position, you will understand why he is likely to be annoyed. In all probability, the goods were shipped in good faith and the mistake was made quite unwittingly, and he will have paid carriage on the boards. Although it may be necessary to insist that he takes them back ultimately, there is always the possibility that the matter can be put right and some allowance be made on the faulty material. If, however, such a material is useless to you at any price, it is wiser to write a courteous letter first, explaining what has happened and asking what arrangements the merchant is prepared to make. This gives the latter a chance to save double carriage, as he may have another customer nearby who would be willing to co-operate by taking the first delivery from you.

Unnecessary Letters

I have already mentioned the importance of avoiding unnecessary correspondence. Few things are likely to irritate a businessman more than letters enclosing invoices, statements and receipts, and letters acknowledging small orders – particularly as the goods probably arrive by the same post.

Nevertheless, there are certain items which do require confirmation; for instance, important telephone calls. Important conversations or decisions should always be confirmed in writing and a copy retained. If this is not done, considerable confusion may later arise. Some business people do not confirm important decisions in this way and in dealing with men of integrity it may be, and usually is, perfectly all right, but the trouble is not only the danger of failing memories but the death of senior officials – and this may lead to serious complications later. In your endeavour to prove your point you may only arouse suspicion in others who do not understand the position if the matter has not been confirmed by letter.

24
Publicity and Sales Letters

Publicity Letters

As its name implies, the purpose of the publicity letter is to obtain publicity for a cause, for a campaign or for merchandise.

As publicity is often a substitute for advertising, and since the latter costs money, it can readily be understood why such publicity is difficult to obtain without involving a certain amount of expense. Editors of papers, magazines and other similar media are constantly on the watch to prevent free publicity being obtained, thereby saving the insertion of a *pro rata* advertisement.

Without going into the technicalities of research on the subject, the importance of publicity is (generally speaking) in direct relation to the reader potential of the medium selected. Thus, to give a simple example, a man selling a product suitable for agricultural use will benefit from publicity in a farming magazine rather than by a display advertisement in a political magazine.

The mention you read in the evening paper about the acreage of orchards owned by a certain cider manufacturer may have been inserted because the editor or journalist considered the information to be of general interest, but more probably it was inserted because the public relations department of the cider farm was able to convince the editor that the matter was of wide appeal.

Again, human nature being what it is, if the firm in question does a lot of advertising in that particular paper, it is possibly correct to suppose that the editor will imagine any information coming from them to be of a more general interest than is in fact the case. Not every publication operates on 100% editorial integrity.

Your best chance of success lies in possessing something that is outstanding in itself and of genuine interest to the public. Remember that the greater the interest you can create, the greater the chance of your particular form of publicity being accepted. To cite an obvious example: a steel manufacturer wishes to increase the use to which his materials can be put and he accordingly initiates a correspondence in the press to the effect that steel should be used in the construction of houses as it is non-inflammable. There is a chance that a timber producer will reply by pointing out that timber can be proofed against fire and that it is much cheaper than steel – each side seeking opportunities for publicity.

You may read that X, the famous film star, has driven a golf ball 250 yards during an International Match at Beverly Hills, California. This statement is probably publicised to draw attention to the film star rather than his prowess as a golfer, and it is more likely that his agent has had a hand in it.

The following gives an example of some publicity issued on behalf of a world-famous jockey, who is on the eve of retirement and whose life story is to be published within a few days. A letter is sent to the editor of a sporting paper with a wide circulation, in the following terms:

Dear Mr Lansell

It occurs to me that you may care to make some reference to one of this country's leading jockeys, John Smith, who is retiring after over thirty years in the saddle.

It is probably not generally known that out of 3,000 races, he has ridden over 700 winning horses and has taken second place in nearly 1,000 races of first-class importance. John will surely be chiefly remembered, however, for his kindness to less fortunate riders and for the unceasing help he has given to the Jockeys' Benevolent Society.

Many of John's admirers will look forward to reading his new book "Keep Your Tail Up", which is to be published on 10 October by Webb & Lockey. In it, much autobiographic information has been included which will appeal not only to turf lovers but also to readers interested in the outstanding figures of the racing world.

Yours sincerely

A press release, giving more detailed information about the book, would also be sent with this letter.

Publicity letters call for endless thought and care if they are to succeed, but it is also easy to over-rate the importance of publicity, for if too much money or time is spent on it, there is less to devote to other and equally important matters.

The Sales Letter

All business executives connected with marketing should be able to write effective sales letters. For some products it will only be necessary to write: "We have pleasure in offering the following:", thereafter listing the individual items, but for others something more will be required. Many letters are damned from the outset by being too long, and the reader becomes bored; alternatively, they are ruined by not being sufficiently explicit. Put yourself in the buyer's place and assess the advantage he would derive from your goods or services, and in your letter come straight to the point and try to show him scientifically and logically why he should have them. Other factors – friendship, sympathy and so on – can play their part, particularly between people who have known one another for a considerable time.

Two examples of sales letters are given here: first a "negative" letter and second a "positive" one which is much better:

Dear Sir

I am writing to make you an offer of our new electronic cash register at £xxx each. Many of our customers have told us how much they like these machines, which are well built and carry with them our One Year Guarantee.

We shall be pleased to arrange for our local representative to call upon you with a machine for trial purposes at any time convenient to you.

Yours faithfully
WOOD & KING LIMITED

A C Wood

Dear Mr Maynard

Our representative was passing your shop last Monday when you were out, and noticed that your assistant was ringing up the goods on an old-fashioned manual cash register. We appreciate that this is fairly general practice in small shops, but wondered if you knew how much time could be saved by using the more modern electronic cash registers?

We have spent many years of research in perfecting the latest type of electronic cash register and we now feel that we have found the answer. Our machines may appear more expensive at the outset, but the extra cost will be more than saved in time and wages. Thanks to the advance of technology in this field in recent years, the cost of these machines has greatly decreased.

Some machines are now so sophisticated that they can keep stock control records, while others use a credit card payment system. Three of our machines are at present in use in a local chemist's shop, and the manager would be happy to answer any questions you might wish to put to him. Our machines are guaranteed for one year but they are likely to give at least ten years' excellent service.

A trial order will be most gratefully received, or our local representative will gladly call and give a demonstration without obligation.

Yours sincerely
WOOD & KING LIMITED

A C Wood

Circulars, Press Releases and Direct Mail Letters

A circular or press release can be sent to announce a social event, can contain up-to-the-minute market reports and information to shareholders, or, of course, can announce a company's new product.

Today, with the advance of computers and word processors, businesses can also send out more "personalised" advertising material. Letters can be written and addressed to individual customers, thereby giving a better impression. However, so many of these direct mail letters are sent out nowadays that many customers barely glance at them before filing them in the waste paper bin!

Firms with a large mail often find it economical to frank their own envelopes; this provides an opportunity to advertise, perhaps, your own trademark or brand.

25

Business Terms, Phrases and Abbreviations

The use of many expressions and terms current in business is, outside certain well-defined limits, to be deprecated. It becomes, in fact, one of those forms of laziness of which we are all guilty.

One of the problems is that different terms apply in different parts of the country or world, even in the same trade, and confusion is likely to arise if some abbreviations are used. This underlines a very important rule: make sure that everything you write is clear.

The letters *E & OE* are seen on quotations, invoices, etc., and stand for an important safeguard: *Errors and Omissions Excepted.* Curiously enough, it is not so often seen today, and I personally deplore its absence as it provides an honorable retreat in the event of a blunder.

Cif stands for *cost, insurance and freight.* If I ask a firm in America to quote me for one ton of cotton, cif Tilbury, his price to me includes the cost of the cargo, the insurance and the freight – the last two of which he prepays. Delivery would be alongside the dock at Tilbury. Unloading charges would be my concern or – to use another business phrase – "for my account".

for means *free on rail,* that is, free delivery as far as the *consignor's* railway station or depot.

fob: free on board, that is, delivered to the ship.

b/l: bill of lading, that is, bill of authority for shipping merchandise by sea.

Dy and *d/d: delivery* and *delivered,* but these words

should be written out in full.

Bulk delivery: delivery only in large quantities.

Each trade has, of course, a host of expressions applicable to its own business.Whilst I do not intend to deal in this book with the hundreds of specialised terms that exist, here is a list of a few of them, together with foreign phrases, which may be met:

List of Some Terms Used in Business

a/c	account
ack.	acknowledge
ad fin.	near or towards the end
ad hoc	for this purpose
ad infinitum	to infinity
ad lib. (ad libitum)	as much as you like; without control
ad referendum	for further consideration
ad valorem (A/V)	based on value – sometimes a Customs & Excise term (or an import duty)
addendum	an additional remark to be added
antedate	date earlier than arranged
AOB	any other business
a/r	all risks
b/e	bill of exchange; also bill of entry (for Customs)
b/f	brought forward (accounts)
bhp	brake horse power
b/l	bill of lading
bleed	the part of an illustration which runs off the page (printing)
Btu	British thermal unit
c/a	current account
CA	Chartered Accountant (Scotland)
c & f	cost and freight
carr. pd.	carriage paid
caveat emptor	let the buyer beware
c/c	centre to centre (measurement)
c.d. (cum dividend)	with the dividend to come
c/f	carried forward (accounts)
cif	cost, insurance and freight
c/o	care of
c.o.d.	cash on delivery
contra	against; opposite (as "contra a/c")
corrigendum	item, word or line to be corrected
cr.	credit or creditor

cu.	cubic
cv	curriculum vitae (life/career history)
cwo	cash with order
D/d	delivered
de facto	in fact
de jure	by right
del credere	risk of a bad debt
dr.	debit or debtor
D.V. (Deo volente)	God willing
D.V. & W.P.	God willing and weather permitting
Dy	Delivery
E & OE	Errors and Omissions excepted
e.g. (exempli gratia)	for example
et al.	and elsewhere
et seq.	and following
etc. (etcetera)	and others
ex	from (as "ex stock")
ex. div.	exclusive of dividend
ex officio	by virtue of office
excl.	exclusive or excluding
fait accompli	an accomplished fact
FAO	for the attention of
fas	free alongside ship
FCA	Fellow of the Institute of Chartered Accountants (England and Wales)
fob	free on board } buyer pays freight after
for	free on rail } put on ship or rail
force majeure	over-riding circumstances, act of God, etc. (whereby a contract may be cancelled or varied)
ft	foot or feet
ft cu	cubic foot or feet
hors de saison	out of season
i.e. (id est)	that is
Inc.	Incorporated (USA equivalent of "limited")
in extenso	at full length
in extremis	at the extreme point
in situ	in position
in status quo	in the original state
in toto	in full
inst.	instant; the present (month)
inter alia	among other matters
inv.	invoice
I.O.U.	I owe you – a promise to repay money, the amount to be stated, signed but not dated
ipso facto	by that very fact
l/c	letter of credit

Ltd	Limited
modus operandi	method of operation
mpg	miles per gallon
mph	miles per hour
ms and mss	manuscript and manuscripts
mv	motor vessel
NB (nota bene)	note well
ne plus ultra	none better
nem. con (nemine contradicente)	without opposition
non seq.	it does not follow
o/a	on account
o/c	overcharge
o/d	overdraft or overdrawn
OHMS	On His/Her Majesty's Service
onus	responsibility
%	per cent or per hundred
op	out of print
O/S	outstanding; also out-size
PA	per annum, yearly; also Personal Assistant
per	by
per diem	by the day
Plc	Public limited company
pod	proof of delivery
post-date	to date in advance – a later date
pp	per pro (on behalf of); also pages
prima facie	as far as first appears – on the face of it
pro	for
pro forma	as a matter of form (pro forma invoice, one calling for cash in advance)
pro rata	proportionately
pro tem.	for the time being
prox. (proximo)	next (month)
PS	post scriptum – written afterwards; an afterthought
PSI	per square inch
qv (quod vide)	which see
R.D.	refer to drawer (e.g. a cheque which a bank will not meet)
rep.	representative
rpm	revolutions per minute
RSVP	please reply
seriatim	serially, one after the other
sine die	indefinitely
sine qua non	a necessity
sq.	square
status quo	existing condition

std.	standard
stet	let it stand; leave as before
sub judice	under consideration, not yet settled in court
tel quel	quality offered just as it is
trs.	transpose
ult. (ultimo)	last (month)
ultra vires	beyond one's powers
VAT	Value Added Tax
verb sap.	a word to the wise is sufficient
verbatim	word for word
via	by way of
vice versa	the other way round
vide	see
viz	namely
w/e	week ending
wef	with effect from
wfi	wait for it
wg	wire gauge
W.P.	word processing; weather permitting
wpb	waste paper basket
wt	weight
∴	therefore

26

Contracts and Employment Agreements

General Remarks

Sufficient importance is rarely attached to contracts or agreements, and the first point I wish to emphasise is that no one should ever sign anything of this nature without reading and understanding it. This sounds childish advice, but I have known otherwise astute men and women who have signed a document unread and lived to regret it bitterly. Contracts or agreements may have long-term results, and, even if entered into through a misunderstanding, are usually irrevocable. The law is frequently an ass but it does have the power of the courts behind it, and indeed, life would not be possible without an undertaking being enforceable. Let rule one be, *read and understand before you sign.*

A contract usually affects two (or more) people or parties, and if all were honourable and reasonable a strongly worded clause would doubtless matter little, as it could be rectified by a new agreement. Unfortunately, in business as elsewhere, there exist people who try to take advantage.

On several occasions I have known instances where contracts for merchandise or services were drawn up on the understanding that the wording was the same as in a previous similar contract. Now, it is time-consuming to read again every clause of a long contract which is supposed to be word for word as before, yet, through not having done so, I have known people to find themselves in the most difficult position. One of the parties had slipped in a word or clause which was not identical with the previous contract and which altered its meaning. In other words, the contract was obtained by sharp practice. So, at the risk of repetition, do not forget rule one – read and understand before you sign.

Were such an unfortunate thing to happen to you, it is, of course, possible that by visiting the dishonest party and "having it out" a fresh contract could be obtained and the "incorrect" one destroyed. It is also possible that if the other party refused to put the matter right, a lawyer could advise you how to escape the dread consequences of your folly by taking advantage of some weak clause in the contract which would make the whole thing unworkable. Were this not possible, if by your carelessness you had signed something which was going to have a serious effect on your life, quite likely it would be worthwhile threatening, or even going so far as to take the matter to court. If the word or words which had been inserted without your knowledge were unreasonable and such as no reasonable person would sign, and if you could swear on oath that the other party had assured you the contract was identical with a previous one between you, my guess is that the Court would declare the second contract null and void. But my guess may be wrong, and in every court battle both sides think they will win, or they would pull out beforehand, and *one side always loses* – remember that before going to law.

I do not wish to leave this vital rule one, *Read and Understand,* until I have hammered it thoroughly, at the risk of your being annoyed with me, into your conscious and subconscious mind, because once you have really grasped it you are fairly safe.

Understanding is most important. A promise made verbally, or in an exchange of letters could easily be just as enforceable as a contract. True, in a verbal promise, if there is no witness, it might be difficult for the other party to enforce the terms, but often it is less difficult than one might think. Another equally vital rule, then, is to be very careful what you do promise. Indeed, one of my business mottoes is "promise as little as you can, but carry out all you do undertake". Remember, make as few definite promises as possible, for they all have to be fulfilled.

Understanding the terms of a contract is often difficult. To give a simple example which comes to mind: I remember a contract which was fixed in January with the shipment date July/August/September. A few days after the contract was made, the buyer asked to have it altered as he found he could not accommodate the earlier shipment dates and he inserted "Shipment: not before September". In his mind he wanted to make sure the goods did not leave in July or August but in September. The shipper, thousands of miles away, apparently read the contract otherwise – intentionally or unintentionally, I do not know – with the outcome that he did not ship until the following December. The buyer could do nothing and had to accept delivery although the material was too late for the job and he was forced to buy at a high price in the open market to fill his order from his own customer, and was subsequently landed with a shipment of specially-cut material which was useless to him. He lost thousands of pounds.

I remember another contract in which an author, in exchange for a considerable advance, was to deliver a manuscript "when complete", no date being mentioned for completion. Need I add it was never delivered and the publisher lost his advance money? The particular author was a crook, and this brings me to the subject of dealing with people lacking in integrity.

No one is clever enough to deal with dishonest people and get away with it for long; the man who is out to "do" you will almost certainly succeed in the end. He spends his time working out clauses which enable him to escape, but which are so worded that you are likely not to notice the weakness in the wording. Avoid, therefore, as far as possible, all contracts with those who are dishonest, however profitable a deal may appear on the face of it.

Many contracts can be "legally" broken and that is why,

although every care should be exercised to make the wording clear and straightforward, it is far better to bank upon the integrity of the person with whom you deal, than on his actual contract. It is because of this that we have the saying: "You can drive a horse and cart through any contract", although it is only partly true.

Many people imagine that lawyers can draw up foolproof contracts, but a little thought will show that this is not so. A lawyer may not understand the intricacies of every trade and whilst he may be able to help the inexperienced in drafting clauses, he may omit or overlook some important point; so much is this so that I consider a solicitor, for this type of work, unless he has special experience in the particular field, not to be particularly useful. As an adviser he may be helpful, but probably less so than some experienced business colleague.

Owing to all the different terms and customs in each trade, I can do little more than give brief outlines here and sound warnings of a general nature.

In this question of understanding, we should be clear what the contract is. It is little more than the setting down, as a permanent record and reference, the terms or conditions which have been agreed between the parties, often after long negotiation and discussion in which give-and-take usually play an important part. The contract is necessary because it saves the memory, and should any of the contracting parties die or retire, acts as a guide to those who follow. If a business is sold, its existing contracts are extremely important and valuable.

The wording should be straightforward. It is not necessary, and indeed it is not "done" today to use big words and legal phrases if ordinary English can be employed. For the normal business contract, legal advice is usually not necessary, but I must say that although I have perused many contracts, I have hardly ever seen a properly worded one. This is, I think, due to the habit of not bringing the wording up-to-date to fit new conditions, many firms using the same old style which served their predecessors well. I will give an example of what I regard as poor wording which I have seen in the publishing trade. "The price of the book will be £20 net and the rate of royalty shall be £2 per copy." This is possibly perfect wording so far as the first edition of the book is concerned, but perceive what an awkward position the publisher has put himself into should the book become a bestseller and go into many editions year after year. Due to rising costs it might no longer be possible for the firm to sell the book at £20 and it might be necessary to raise the price to £30. If the author is fair, it should be easy enough to obtain his agreement, either by a new contract or by exchange of letters, which is as legal, that the price should be £30 and the royalty rate £3 (which is the same percentage), but what could happen is that the author disagrees, or perhaps he or she has died and the widow or widower is an unreasonable person, so that the publisher is faced with the probability of losing the rights of publishing the book to some competing firm who will enjoy all the spade work he has done in establishing it.

If he had worded the original clause as follows he would not be in this predicament:

"The Publisher expects the price of the book will be £20 for the first edition, but the question of price for the first or any subsequent editions (if any) shall be left entirely to the discretion of the publisher, and the royalty rate *shall be ten per cent* of the net published price."

Of course, there might have to be special clauses about a lower rate of royalty should a paperback book be published, or a cheap edition, or should the book be remaindered, and so on, but I am only using the one clause as illustration of the care which is essential.

I am anxious to stress that those who draw up contracts must think hard of all possibilities and difficulties which may arise, and protect themselves against being "caught out" by some change of circumstances. Clarity is not enough; foresight is also required.

Each party to a contract must protect himself to the best of his ability; this does not mean at all that each is out to catch the other, but an undertaking is a serious matter and should not be lightly given, otherwise the individual's reputation will soon be in question, if he is not ruined.

In manufactured goods it is often possible to make definite promises as to specification, etc., but in other matters – for instance the quantity of hay to be delivered from a field – it may be impossible to be exact, and such difficulties can usually be overcome to everyone's satisfaction by careful wording of the relevant clause. The hay may be cut, and your experienced eye may estimate that it will yield 30 tons. Instead of giving your word to deliver 30 tons, you can say "all the hay in the Long Meadow to be delivered, and the quantity expected to be about 30 tons". This protects you if it turns out to be 23 or 34 tons.

Conditions

On the reverse of most printers' quotations which I receive are printed the following conditions. These are good, from the seller's viewpoint, and therefore bad from mine, although, to be fair, were I a printer I would use them, because of the protection they give. I wrote to the British Printing Industries Federation asking for permission to quote them here, which they have graciously granted. Study the clauses carefully and observe how strongly protected the supplier is. Of course the customer could, if he wished, insist on the elimination of any of the clauses, provided he did so and got the printer to agree before he gave his order. Certain circumstances might arise where it was necessary for one's own protection to insist on one or other of these clauses being inoperative so far as a particular order was concerned.

Here are the conditions:

Conditions of Estimate

1. PRICE VARIATION – Estimates are based on the printer's current costs of production and, unless otherwise agreed, are subject to amendment on or at any time after

acceptance to meet any rise or fall in such costs.

2. TAX – Except in the case of a customer who is not contracting in the course of a business nor holding himself out as doing so, the printer reserves the right to charge the amount of any VAT payable whether or not included on the estimate or invoice.

3. PRELIMINARY WORK – All work carried out, whether experimentally or otherwise, at customer's request will be charged.

4. PROOFS – Proofs of all work may be submitted for customer's approval and the printer shall incur no liability for any errors not corrected by the customer in proofs so submitted. Customer's alterations and additional proofs necessitated thereby shall be charged extra. When style, type or layout is left to the printer's judgment, changes therefrom made by the customer shall be charged extra.

5. DELIVERY AND PAYMENT – (a) Delivery of work shall be accepted when tendered and thereupon or, if earlier, on notification that the work has been completed the ownership shall pass and payment shall become due.

(b) Unless otherwise specified the price quoted is for delivery of the work as set out in the estimate. A charge may be made to cover any extra costs involved for delivery to a different address.

(c) Should expedited delivery be agreed an extra cost may be charged to cover any overtime or any other additional costs involved.

(d) Should work be suspended at the request of or delayed through any default of the customer for a period of 30 days the printer shall then be entitled to payment for work already carried out, materials specially ordered and other additional costs including storage.

6. VARIATIONS IN QUANTITY – Every endeavour will be made to deliver the correct quantity ordered, but estimates are conditional upon margins of 5% for work in one colour only and 10% for other work being allowed for overs or shortage, the same to be charged or deducted.

7. CLAIMS – Advice of damage, delay or partial loss of goods in transit or of non-delivery must be given in

writing to the printer and the carrier within three clear days of delivery (or, in the case of non-delivery, within 28 days of despatch of the goods) and any claim in respect thereof must be made in writing to the printer and the carrier within seven clear days of delivery (or, in the case of non-delivery, within 42 days of despatch). All other claims must be made in writing to the printer within 28 days of delivery. The printer shall not be liable in respect of any claim unless the aforementioned requirements have been complied with except in any particular case where the customer proves that (i) it was not possible to comply with the requirements and (ii) advice (where required) was given and the claim made as soon as reasonably possible.
8. LIABILITY – The printer shall not be liable for any loss to the customer arising from delay in transit not caused by the printer.
9. STANDING MATTER – (a) Metal, film, glass and other materials owned by the printer and used by him in the production of type, plates, moulds, stereotypes, electrotypes, film-setting, negatives, positives, and the like shall remain his exclusive property. Such items when supplied by the customer shall remain the customer's property.

(b) Type may be distributed and lithographic, photogravure, or other work effaced immediately after the order is executed unless written arrangements are made to the contrary. In the latter event, rent may be charged.
10. CUSTOMER'S PROPERTY – (a) Except in the case of a customer who is not contracting in the course of a business nor holding himself out as doing so, customer's property and all property supplied to the printer by or on behalf of the customer shall while it is in the possession of the printer or in transit to or from the customer be deemed to be at customer's risk unless otherwise agreed and the customer should insure accordingly.

(b) The printer shall be entitled to make a reasonable charge for the storage of any customer's property left with the printer before receipt of the order or after notification to the customer of completion of the work.

11. MATERIAL SUPPLIED BY CUSTOMER – (a) The printer may reject any paper, plates or other materials supplied or specified by the customer which appear to him to be unsuitable. Additional cost incurred if materials are found to be unsuitable during production may be charged, except that if the whole of any part of such additional cost could have been avoided but for unreasonable delay by the printer in ascertaining the unsuitability of the materials then that amount shall not be charged to the customer.

(b) Where materials are so supplied or specified, the printer will take every care to secure the best results, but responsibility will not be accepted for imperfect work caused by defects in or unsuitability of materials so supplied or specified.

(c) Quantities of materials supplied shall be adequate to cover normal spoilage.

12. INSOLVENCY – If the customer ceases to pay his debts in the ordinary course of business or cannot pay his debts as they become due or being a company is deemed to be unable to pay its debts or has a winding-up petition issued against it or being a person commits an act of bankruptcy or has a bankruptcy petition issued against him, the printer without prejudice to other remedies shall

(i) have the right not to proceed further with the contract or any other work for the customer and be entitled to charge for work already carried out (whether completed or not) and materials purchased for the customer, such charge to be an immediate debt due to him, and

(ii) in respect of all unpaid debts due from the customer have a general lien on all goods and property in his possession (whether worked on or not) and shall be entitled on the expiration of 14 days' notice to dispose of such goods or property in such manner and at such price as he thinks fit and to apply the proceeds towards such debts.

13. ILLEGAL MATTER – (a) The printer shall not be required to print any matter which in his opinion is or may be of an illegal or libellous nature or an infringement of the proprietary or other rights of any third party.

(b) The printer shall be indemnified by the customer in respect of any claims, costs and expenses arising out of any libellous matter or of any infringement of copyright, patent, design, or of any proprietary or personal rights contained in any material printed for the customer. The indemnity shall extend to any amounts paid on a lawyer's advice in settlement of any claim.

14. PERIODICAL PUBLICATIONS – A contract for the printing of periodical publications may not be terminated by either party unless written notice is given as follows:

Nature of Publication	*Length of Notice* (given at any time)
Weekly) Fortnightly) Monthly)	13 weeks
Two monthly) Quarterly)	26 weeks

Nevertheless the printer may terminate any such contract forthwith should any sum due thereunder remain unpaid.

15. FORCE MAJEURE – The printer shall be under no liability if he shall be unable to carry out any provision of the contract for any reason beyond his control including (without limiting the foregoing) Act of God, legislation, war, fire, flood, drought, failure of power supply, lock-out, strike or other action taken by employees in contemplation or furtherance of a dispute or owing to any inability to procure materials required for the performance of the contract. During the continuance of such a contingency the customer may by written notice to the printer elect to terminate the contract and pay for work done and materials used, but subject thereto shall otherwise accept delivery when available.

16. LAW – These Conditions and all other express terms of the contract shall be governed and construed in accordance with the laws of England.

I shall make no further comment on these excellent conditions.

Another point to remember is that any clause in a contract which would make the other party or yourself break the law is not enforceable – that is, you cannot contract outside the framework of the current law of the land.

Contracts

I will now draw up an imaginary contract between an author and a publisher, and later comment on the different clauses. This is for guidance only and should not necessarily be used as it stands.

MEMORANDUM OF THE AGREEMENT made this *ninth* day of *September* in the year xxxx between *Mr William John Blask,* of *71 First Street, Watford, Hertfordshire, WA1 7YY* (hereinafter called the Author) of the one part, and *Blank & Blank Limited* of *24 Terminus Road, London, WC2A 7UU* (hereinafter called the Publisher) of the other part.

IT IS AGREED between the Author and the Publisher as follows regarding the manuscript now completed and at present called *"Fun and Games":*

1. The Author assigns to the Publisher the copyright of the material under the terms of this Agreement and the right to publish it in book form throughout the world. In the event of publication either in the United States of America or in a foreign language, it is understood that the Author shall receive 50% (fifty per centum) and the Publisher 50% (fifty per centum) of any royalties, profits or outright sum received for any licence to publish granted by the Publisher. It is further agreed that the Publisher shall not protect the copyright in the United States of America against piracy as he does not consider this worth

the cost in view of the normally remote chance of such piracy.

2. It is expected that the first edition shall be large, publication to be as soon as possible, to be printed on good quality paper, bound in cloth (or imitation cloth), price expected to be £20 (twenty pounds) but left to the discretion of the Publisher; subsequent editions to be in the original form or in such other form or at such price as he may decide in relation to existing market conditions. The Author shall retain a copy of the manuscript for safety, which is to be delivered to the Publisher should he so request.

3. The Publisher shall submit to the Author proof sheets of the first edition and of subsequent editions, or, in the event of the Author's decease, to his Executors, and the work of careful revision shall be promptly carried out. Failing agreement with the Executors, the Publisher reserves the right to employ an outside expert and shall deduct the cost from royalties. It is understood that the cost of corrections, to the extent that this exceeds 10% (ten per centum) of the cost of composition, shall be met by the Author.

4. The Author warrants the Publisher that the said work is in no way a violation of any existing copyright and that it contains nothing obscene, objectionable, indecent or libellous and will indemnify the Publisher for any loss, injury or damage, including any legal costs or expense properly incurred by the Publisher, in consequence of any breach of this warranty.

5. The Publisher shall pay to the Author a royalty of 10% (ten per centum) on the published price of any and every copy sold. On export sales the royalty shall be at half rate. If the book has to be remaindered at less than one quarter of the retail price no royalty shall be payable on copies remaindered.

6. Should extracts be taken from the book, any monies accruing therefrom shall be divided between the Author and Publisher, the former receiving 50% (fifty per centum) and the latter the balance 50% (fifty per centum).

7. Should the book be allowed to go out of print for more than eighteen months, all rights herein granted shall revert to the Author after six months' notice is given in writing to the Publisher, without prejudice to any monies due.

8. The Publisher shall render to the Author an account during November in each year (or within three months thereafter) after the date of publication and the amount shown to be due in royalties shall be paid to the Author at the time such account is rendered. Should accounts and payments not be so rendered, this Contract shall be cancelled and all rights shall revert to the Author without prejudice to monies due.

9. The Publisher hereby agrees to distribute review copies of the said book and to give six voucher copies to the Author on publication.

10. The Publisher reserves the right to carry out minor editing.

11. As the Publisher expects to spend a considerable amount on publicity, he hopes that the Author will give him first refusal of any other work proposed by him in book form.

12. It is understood that no similar book shall be written by the Author and published elsewhere which could conflict with the sales of the aforementioned book during the life of this Contract.

13. It is agreed that the Author through his or her accountants or solicitors shall have the right of access to the sales record of the Publisher to verify the sales figures.

14. The rights and obligations under this agreement shall be binding upon the Author and Publisher respectively and shall belong to and be binding upon the personal representatives and assigns of the Author and the successors in title and assigns of the Author respectively.

15. The Publisher retains the right before publication, to amend or in extreme cases to cancel this Contract in the event of any Government action or interference which would make the completion of the undertaking impracticable.

AS WITNESS the hands of the parties this *ninth* day of *September* xxxx.

Signature of Author/Publisher
Signature of Witness
Occupation of Witness
Address of Witness

Comments

A copy of the contract is retained while the original is away to be signed by the author, his signature being witnessed. When the signed original returns, the copy, this time signed by the publisher and witnessed, is sent to the author for his retention. This is known as exchanging contracts and is often done in the publisher's office or the home of the author.

The contract given above is a simple one; obviously a manuscript which has not been written requires different wording, as do manuscripts which have to contain illustrations – questions such as who is to pay for the reproduction rights of photographs and so on should be dealt with in the contract and not left to "mutual agreement" as is so often done and which frequently ends in misunderstanding and disagreement.

CLAUSE 1 – By obtaining the copyright instead of merely the right to publish for a given number of years, the publisher is in a stronger position. The percentages to be divided in the event of overseas publication might be disputed by the author, but the publisher could defend himself on the grounds that but for his initial risk and expense the book would probably never be published abroad, and also he has considerable expense in trying to market the average book overseas. The USA is probably the most important market for British books but foreign language translations are important as well, and the remarks are merely inserted to prevent any misunderstanding. Possibly a well-known author with the likelihood of US publication might wish his American copyright to be protected by a special process, which can be done, or some authors might refuse to grant USA rights.

CLAUSE 2 – Notice that the publisher does not commit himself to the size of the edition, nor to produce the book at an exact price. This gives him the chance to protect himself if conditions alter during the time taken for production; for instance, he might originally have intended to publish 5,000 copies, but before the final proofs are returned to the printer, a slump might have set in for the particular type of book, so that he could reduce the quantity to, say, 2,000 copies. He also leaves himself free as to future prices or format. The clause insisting on a copy for safety gives him real protection in the event of loss or damage to the original manuscript during the production stage. Fires can occur in printing works, and in the absence of this clause the publisher might find himself seriously out of pocket.

CLAUSE 3 – The publisher protects himself against executors, who in such a matter can be unco-operative. Care is taken in the event of the author carrying out an unreasonable number of corrections; a specific figure is inserted (and it is probably wise as it saves argument).

CLAUSE 4 – An interesting clause because it is of

doubtful legality, and possibly could not be enforced in law, since if, for example, libel is included in the book, the publisher and even the printer are legally responsible, as well as the author. But the clause probably has a deterrent effect on an over-bold author, and is a customary one.

CLAUSE 5 – The reason for the nil royalty if the book gets remaindered is because in this circumstance the publisher has lost badly on the book anyway.

CLAUSE 6 – Self explanatory.

CLAUSES 7 and 8 – These, as can be seen, give good protection to both author and publisher. Always remember there are two sides to every contract, and the perfect contract from the viewpoint of one party would be unfair to the other, so all contracts are really a compromise, but *your* aim must be to secure all the safeguards you possibly can, and, as mentioned above, never promise what there is doubt about your being able to fulfil.

CLAUSES 9 and 10 – Self-explanatory.

CLAUSE 11 – Some publishers insist on first refusal of the next three books, while others request first refusal of all future books. Personally, I prefer to hope the author will play fair, and I always feel that the more you try to tie him to you, the keener he will be to break away. Indeed, it is doubtful if such a clause could be enforced in law unless it was much more tightly worded to cover all sorts of matters such as royalty rate, advances, if any, and so forth.

CLAUSE 12 – This is self-protection for the publisher, but some authors will not agree to it except with modifications.

CLAUSE 13 – Often a customary clause in the publishing trade.

CLAUSE 14 – Protection for both sides, and necessary in a long-term contract such as the one under discussion.

CLAUSE 15 – An emergency clause for the publisher's protection. This clause is probably unnecessary, as I believe all contracts are subject to cancellation or alteration when something arises which can properly be termed "an act of God", or a cause of some kind beyond the parties' control.

Although the foregoing is a simple contract, several lessons can be learned from the care with which the clauses have to be drawn up.

Read, re-read, sleep on and think over all clauses in a contract – but do not forget no one can cover every possible combination of contingencies, and perhaps, with life so short, it is as well.

Giving Notice Under a Contract

Let us assume that the book referred to in the above has been allowed to go out of print for a period of over 18 months; what should the author do? In practice he would probably visit or write a friendly letter to the publisher to ask the position, and often such matters are handled in that friendly manner with excellent results.

Sometimes, however, an author meets with a "difficult" publisher; in other words, the one party to a contract may find he does not get on well with the other party, for some reason or other, and wishes to take advantage of the clause. When this occurs, things are less easy. If the other party is a small private partnership concern, a carefully worded letter, referring to the contract, giving its date and referring to the appropriate clause by number, would be sent by registered post to the senior partner with a request for acknowledgement. In the case of a limited company, the correct procedure would be to write to the Company Secretary. Something on the following lines would meet either case in our sample contract:

Dear Sir

I refer to our contract dated 9 September XXXX for the publication entitled "Fun and Games". I understand this book has been out of print for eighteen months, and I hereby exercise the option to terminate the said contract under Clause 7. Please treat this as the necessary six months' notice in writing requisite for the exercise of the said option without prejudice to any monies due to me. I shall thereafter consider myself free to arrange for publication elsewhere.

Please confirm termination of contract in accordance with this letter.

Yours faithfully

Non-Fulfilment of Contract

What happens if one party feels the other side has not fulfilled a contract? Normally, unless there is any clause to the contrary, a contract or agreement is enforceable in courts of law. What can be said, however, is that going to law on such a matter can be expensive and is rarely to be recommended. Quite often the hint of legal action will be enough to make the other party see reason, but remember it may be you who is being unreasonable; so many of us, when faced with our own problems, cannot see the other side's viewpoint. Damages awarded for a breach of contract may be heavy; amounts depend on what is involved.

In many trades a system of arbitration has been evolved when disagreement arises, so as to eliminate the cost of litigation; but like all substitutes for the real thing, the system has its faults. Among them is the fact that it is sometimes hard to find someone of knowledge, integrity and impartiality who is acceptable to both sides, if it is a case of appointing a sole arbitrator. If an arbitrator has to be appointed by each side, with an umpire, then costs are already running up. Since an arbitrator is within his rights in demanding his fee before announcing his verdict, the shock to the loser is frequently considerable, if slightly delayed.

On the whole, I think it is better to have an ordinary contract which can be taken before a court of justice if the need arises, but some may prefer the arbitration method. Where the latter is used, I think it only wise to include some precaution in the clause as a protection; for example:

> "Any dispute that shall arise between the parties hereto with reference to this Agreement or the construction thereof or any matter contained in or arising out of this Agreement shall be referred to the arbitration of two persons (one to be named by each party) or to a mutually agreed umpire in accordance with the provisions of the Arbitration Act 1950, or any amending or substitute statute for the time being in force or alternatively at the option of either party, to be declared beforehand, recourse to normal Courts of Justice may be adopted."

Depending upon what is at stake, at least the option of going before a court is available. In practice, many will risk an arbitration, but if you insist on going to Court, if you have a good case, you will probably win a settlement out of court before the hearing starts. Few firms like the publicity of being sued.

Employment Agreements or Contracts

In England and Wales an employer is not obliged to give an employee a written contract of employment, but is required not later than two months after the beginning of the employee's appointment, to give the employee a written statement which details those particulars that are required by law.

Although a written contract is not a legal requirement it is good practice to put in writing what you have agreed with your employee because if a dispute arises you will be able to refer to it to help settle the matter.

This statement must give particulars of the terms and conditions of employment, as follows:

Rate of pay, dates on which pay is paid, and job title.
Normal hours of work and entitlement to lunch-hour and other breaks.
Holiday entitlement.
Procedure for making up pay during illness, if any.
Whether there is a pension scheme.
Length of notice of termination to which the employee is entitled. By law the entitlements are:

1. After four weeks' employment – one week's notice.
2. For each year of continuous employment between two and twelve years – one week's notice for each year.
3. For continuous employment of twelve years or more – twelve weeks' notice.

Procedure for taking up grievances and disciplinary complaints.
Disciplinary rules.

Example of a Statement of Employment

In this statement under the Contracts of Employments Acts, XXX Company gives you, ... of .... particulars of the terms and conditions on which it is employing you with effect from the ....

1. Your initial rate of pay is £............ per month. You will be paid on the 25th day of each month.

2. Your normal hours of work are .... per week. Your daily hours are .... You are entitled to a one-hour mid-day meal break, 12.30 p.m. to 1.30 p.m. or at a different time by agreement.

3. In addition to Public Holidays and the other days on which the Office is closed at Christmas time, your holiday entitlement is three working weeks per

calendar year. Dates are to be settled as far in advance as possible with the Manager. On the completion of three years' service you become entitled to an additional one working week's holiday per year, provided that this latter is taken during the Winter months October to April.

4. In addition, the Directors always give favourable consideration to requests for extra holidays without pay.

5. EITHER
   The Company will continue to make up your normal pay during any unavoidable absence during sickness.

   OR
   The Company will pay you statutory sick pay in accordance with the law, provided that you comply with the Company's rules and regulations as regards the notification of such illness, and the provision of the necessary doctor's certificate, details of which are available from your Manager.

6. The Company does not provide a pension scheme.

7. You are entitled to receive one week's notice of termination after four weeks' employment; one week's notice for each year of continuous employment between two and twelve years, and twelve weeks' notice if the period of continuous employment is twelve years or more. You are required to give the Company one week's notice of termination, but longer if possible.

8. The title of your job is ....

9. Disciplinary rules: These are kept to the minimum, but the Company cannot employ those who break them.

(a) You are not allowed to enter the premises outside working hours.
(b) You are not allowed to smoke on the premises.
(c) You are not allowed to use the Company's postage stamps for private purposes.
(d) You are not allowed to use the fire hose for any purpose except putting out a fire.
(e) You must ask the Manager's permission if you wish to:
  (1) make a private telephone call;
  (2) use the photocopier for private purposes;
  (3) purchase items of stationery, wrapping materials, etc.
  (4) purchase stock;

  and if permission is given, you must:
  (i) be as brief as possible on the telephone;
  (ii) pay for calls made or materials used or bought, at cost;
  (iii) do private work only during the lunch hour.

10. If at any time you are dissatisfied with any disciplinary decision affecting you, you may make a complaint to any of the Directors who are in the Office at the time.

11. If you have any individual grievance relating to your employment here, the procedure is for you to raise it with the Manager. If you are still dissatisfied, the procedure is then for you to raise the matter with any of the Company Directors who are in the Office at the time.

In addition you may wish to restrain your employees from competing with you or poaching your customers for a reasonable period after the end of the employment. Drafting enforceable clauses for this purpose is complex and should be dealt with by a lawyer.

Some employees may want complicated service

contracts, which might be very difficult and expensive to break. I would advise strongly against these, initially at any rate. Give your employees the ordinary length of termination of notice as required by law, but no more.

At a later date, a loyal employee might feel he deserves a better service contract, but it should be considered later, rather than earlier.

Job Title

It is important to give careful thought to a job title. The consequences of a badly chosen title can be far reaching. For example, under the law, if a woman with more than two years' service, takes maternity leave, provision must be made for her to return to a similar, although not necessarily identical, position as she held before.

If you want further advice without having to consult a lawyer, excellent self-help legal packs which include the Contract of Employment form and instruction booklet are available from larger stationers.

Index